Practical Exercises in Pharmacy Law and Ethics

Second edition

Gordon E Appelbe

LL B, PhD, MSc, BSc(Pharm), FRPharmS, FCPP, HonMPS(Aus)

Joy Wingfield

LL M, MPhil, BPharm, FRPharmS, Dip Ag Vet Pharm, FCPP

Lindsay M Taylor

BSc, MA, MRPharmS

London • Chicago   **Pharmaceutical Press**

Published by the Pharmaceutical Press
Publications division of the Royal Pharmaceutical Society of Great Britain

1 Lambeth High Street, London SE1 7JN
100 South Atkinson Road, Suite 206, Grayslake, IL 60030-7820, USA

© jointly by Gordon E Appelbe, Joy Wingfield,
Lindsay M Taylor and the Pharmaceutical Press, 2002

First published 1997
Second edition 2002

Text design by Barker/Hilsdon, Lyme Regis, Dorset
Typeset by Photoprint, Torquay, Devon
Printed in Great Britain by TJ International, Padstow, Cornwall

ISBN 0 85369 522 9

A catalogue record for this book is available from the British
Library.

Practical

Exercises in

Pharmacy

DATE DUE FOR RETURN

This book may be recalled before the above date.

This book may be recalled before the above date.

Gordon E Appelbe, LL B, PhD, MSc, BSc(Pharm), FRPharmS, FCPP, HonMPS (Aus), is an independent pharmaceutical/legal consultant. He qualified as a pharmacist in 1956 and then worked for nine years in community pharmacy. He joined the staff of the Pharmaceutical Society in 1965, first as an inspector under the Pharmacy Acts and then, in 1971, as secretary to the Statutory Committee. He was appointed deputy head of the Law Department in 1974 and was head of the Law Department and Chief Inspector from 1978 to 1991.

Joy Wingfield, LL M, MPhil, BPharm, FRPharmS, Dip Ag Vet Pharm, FCPP, is Boots Special Professor of Pharmacy Law and Ethics at the University of Nottingham and a pharmacy practice consultant for Boots The Chemists Ltd. She qualified as a pharmacist in 1971 and then worked for five years in community pharmacy. She joined the staff of the Pharmaceutical Society in 1976 as an inspector under the Pharmacy Acts. From 1986 until 1991 she was the senior administrator, and later head of Ethics Division in the Law Department, responsible for professional and registration matters. This was followed by nine years as the assistant pharmacy superintendent for Boots. She now occupies a part-time chair as Boots special professor in pharmacy law and ethics at Nottingham University and retains a part-time practice consultancy for Boots The Chemists.

Lindsay M Taylor BSc, MA, MRPharmS, was Boots Teacher Practitioner in the School of Pharmacy, De Monfort University, Leicester for almost ten years. She took up the new post of Clinical Governance and NHS Information Manager at the head office of Lloydspharmacy in September 1999. She undertakes research and writing activities as well as being responsible for instigating a wide variety of NHS initiatives throughout the Company. She qualified as a pharmacist in 1973 and then worked for 17 years in community pharmacy as a relief manager, locum tenens, and part-time pharmacist. She was a teacher, tutor and examinations officer at Groby Community College from 1982 to 1990.

Contents

■ **Level 2**

The questions are grouped in sections, as indicated below, according to the legislation they cover. The order of topic areas is the same as for Level 1. An asterisk next to the description of the question indicates that it is a multiple-choice question. The number of asterisks indicates the classification of possible answers.

The Medicines Act

1 Who decides what is an emergency?
The weekend visit of the mother who has diabetes 137

2 Rational decisions: palliative care versus drug abuse
The clumsy toddler and the spilt medicines 145

3 A real emergency
The teenager and the coleslaw salad 151

4 Recycling medicines for the Third World
The priest in Ethiopia 157

5 Protecting the reputation of the profession
The residential home and the 'rogue' tablets 163

6 Responsibility for the supply of unlicensed medicines
The child and the Phenergan Elixir 169

7 Responsibility for the supply of unlicensed medicines (2)
The midnight telephone call from the neonatal ward 177

8 The NHS contract; responsibilities of the superintendent
The blizzard in the Yorkshire Dales 185

9 Duty to protect the public, even from pharmacists
The locum and the bottle of whisky 191

10 Duty to protect the public, even from pharmacists (2)
The European locum and the hospital staff 197

11 Duty to protect the public, even from other healthcare professionals
The contraindication and the confident practice nurse 205

12 Accountabilities of an employee; duties of a superintendent
The non-pharmacist manager and the sales of codeine linctus 213

13 A matter of confidentiality
The suicide and his girlfriend 219

14 A matter of confidentiality (2)
The friend in hospital and her anxious mother 225

15 Private beliefs and patients' needs
The adolescent girl and the Levonelle 231

Preface

Practical Exercises in Pharmacy Law and Ethics is a companion volume to the textbook Dale and Appelbe's *Pharmacy Law and Ethics*. Unless indicated otherwise, the cross-references in this book refer to the seventh edition of *Pharmacy Law and Ethics* (2001). The authors' aim is to provide undergraduates, preregistration students and practising pharmacists with problem-solving exercises that enable them to increase their understanding of pharmacy law and ethics. After working through the text, readers should be able to present cogent arguments in answer both to examination questions and the problems raised in situations drawn from the practice of community pharmacy.

Whether you are an undergraduate student just starting to learn about the laws that affect how pharmacists carry out their everyday duties, a preregistration graduate, or an experienced pharmacist with years of professional expertise and knowledge, you will inevitably encounter problems to which you do not know the answer. This companion volume gives examples of such questions, at all levels, together with explanations of how the answer is reached. If you are a preregistration student anticipating the demands of the registration examination, or a pharmacist returning or changing to practising in community pharmacy, we hope to help you develop skills and acquire knowledge that enable you to solve problems – whether for an examination or a 'real-life' situation – that demand a knowledge of pharmacy law and ethics.

We wish to express our thanks to our publishers, particularly Charles Fry, Paul Weller and John Wilson for their enthusiasm for, and encouragement of, our efforts. Thanks are also due to pharmacy colleagues, Rachel Kenward, Sandra Beatty, Nisha Pounj, Surinder Bassan and Caryl Kelly for their ideas and second opinions, and to Gerald Prince of the Department of Pharmaceutical Sciences, De Montfort University, Leicester, for the valuable help received. Responsibility for the text and any views expressed therein lies with the authors.

Gordon E Appelbe, Joy Wingfield, Lindsay M Taylor

April 2002

Introduction

Although *Practical Exercises in Pharmacy Law and Ethics* can be used as a 'stand-alone' book, you may find it helpful to refer to the accompanying textbook – Dale and Appelbe's *Pharmacy Law and Ethics* – to find out what the law says. That book describes, in the appropriate terminology, various aspects of British law that affect pharmacists. However, to practise as a pharmacist you will need to understand and be able to apply these laws. Pharmacists at all levels can find it quite difficult to apply the concepts to a typical pharmacy situation – this is where this book can help you.

Questions on 'real-life' situations are presented and answered, with explanations, later in the appropriate section. You will need to think carefully about how best to use the book to help yourself. If you are just learning about a new topic, we recommend 'having a go' for yourself first, using the main text where indicated, and referring to the answers and explanation when you get stuck. Alternatively, if you are preparing for an examination, it is probably better to give yourself some practice and to do the whole question or section without referring to the answers, but making a note to look up and revise any topics that you find difficult.

The questions are set at three levels as follows:

Level 1 is mainly for undergraduates and covers pharmacy law.
Level 2 is for undergraduates and preregistration students, and covers both pharmacy law and ethics.

Level 3 is for registered pharmacists, can be tackled earlier in training, and explores professional decision-making in practice situations.

Within each level, the questions are graded so that the earlier ones, which are explained very thoroughly, are at the beginning of the section and those that could be used to test yourself for examination questions are at the end. Within each level, the type of questions set will vary, and include short-answer questions, multiple-choice questions and, in the case of Level 3, practice situations. In some cases the questions are linked so that, for example, pharmacists returning to practice and who are aware of the need to revise their knowledge of the sale of prescribed dangerous substances and fireworks can test themselves on the law at Level 1, the ethics at Level 2 and the decision-making procedure at Level 3.

We hope you will find the approach useful to your studies, at whatever level.

What you will learn, in formal terms, at each level

- ### Level 1

Learning objective

To enable you, using Dale and Appelbe's *Pharmacy Law and Ethics*, and other reference sources where appropriate, to answer questions that test your knowledge of pharmacy law.

Learning outcomes

On completing Level 1 you should:

- Understand some of the reasons for the introduction of the Medicines Act 1968.
- Have a basic grasp of the scope and administration of the Medicines Act, including the definitions used.
- Be aware of the constraints placed upon the development, testing and marketing of medicinal products by the Medicines Act.
- Understand the licensing procedures of the Medicines Act (and the exemptions for some substances under certain conditions) and the role of the Inspectorate.
- Be fully conversant with the exact conditions under which GSL, P and POM medicinal products can be sold and supplied to the general public and professionals.
- Be fully conversant with the exact conditions under which controlled drugs can be sold and supplied to the general public and professionals.

- Be fully conversant with the exact conditions that apply to the sale and supply of poisons, prescribed dangerous substances and spirits to the general public and to professionals.

■ Level 2

Learning objective

To enable you, using Dale and Appelbe's *Pharmacy Law and Ethics*, and other reference sources where appropriate, to answer questions that test your knowledge of pharmacy law and the principles and guidance of the Code of Ethics.

Learning outcomes

On completing Level 2 you should:
- Be able to apply the Code of Ethics to simple situations and to understand the significance of its principles, obligations, guidance and standards.
- Have a working knowledge of the structure of the NHS and the function of the various bodies, and understand the differences between the English, Scottish and Welsh systems.
- Have a working knowledge of the Health and Safety at Work etc. Act 1974 and other miscellaneous legislation affecting pharmacy.
- Have a deeper understanding of the implications of the Code of Ethics for practising pharmacists and the consequences of contravening its philosophy to pharmacy as a profession.

■ Level 3

Learning objective

To enable you to gain a deeper understanding, through a problem-solving approach, of professional decision-making, drawing on moral philosophy and other knowledge as well as information from Dale and Appelbe's *Pharmacy Law and Ethics*.

Learning outcomes

On completing Level 3 you should:
- Be able to analyse a complex situation and identify questions of law, ethics and professional good practice.
- Be able to adopt a systematic approach to reaching reasoned decisions on professional practice problems.

- Understand those areas of decision-making which are subject to legal or other rules and those which are matters of professional judgement.
- Understand the range of knowledge – clinical, professional, legal and personal – which must be assembled as the basis for sound professional decision-making.

1

Level One

The history of the development of current legislation that affects pharmacists

The laws that affect community pharmacists today have evolved from many previous Acts of parliament governing the sale of poisons and dangerous substances; for each of the Acts listed below, describe very briefly the controls that were put in place by the legislation.

1˙   The Poisons and Pharmacy Act 1908.
2   The International Opium Convention, which led to the Dangerous Drugs Act 1920.
3   The Therapeutic Substances Act 1925.
4   The Pharmacy and Poisons Act 1933.
5   The 1972 Poisons Act.

What issues should I consider?

- Think of any milestones of drug therapy that you might know from general knowledge – the introduction of insulin and penicillin and the development and use of synthetic compounds due to advances in chemical knowledge would be good examples.
- Also consider historical events such as world wars and the increasing 'social' use of drugs that have led to changes in how drugs are used (and abused).
- The laws that you are asked to find out about in this question were largely introduced in response to such changes and arose from the recognition that controls needed to be introduced to restrict the availability and control the quality of increasingly potent substances.

Where should I look in Pharmacy Law & Ethics?

The Introduction describes the development of the laws that affect community pharmacists today, together with some of the reasons for their introduction.

Answers and Explanations

1

1   The Poisons and Pharmacy Act 1908 extended the list of poisons and allowed licensed dealers as well as pharmacists to sell them. The Act also gave the conditions under which a 'body corporate' or a company, rather than an individual, could carry on the business of a chemist and druggist.

2   International agreement on the control of narcotics, known as the International Opium Convention (which led to the Dangerous Drugs Act 1920), followed the use of strong painkillers based on opium in the First World War.

3   In 1922 insulin was discovered; diabetics being treated with the substance needed to know the amount of activity, but it could not be assayed and the quality controlled by the chemical means available at the time. The Therapeutic Substances Act 1925 controlled the manufacture of such substances.

4   The Pharmacy and Poisons Act 1933 introduced to the practice of pharmacy many fundamental changes, some of which are recognisable in today's legislation. An example would be the introduction of substances which could only be supplied to the public on prescription, in much the same way as the Prescription Only Medicines (POMs) of today.

5   Before the Medicines Act 1968, many medicines were classified as poisons and controlled by appropriate legislation. With the introduction of legislation specifically designed for medicines, non-medicinal poisons had to be controlled separately - hence the Poisons Act 1972.

Question 2

The scope and administration of the Medicines Act

The implications of the general principle – that every activity to do with medicines is under the jurisdiction of the Medicines Act – is considered briefly in this question.

Decide whether each of the following statements is true or false. You might also like to make a note of any reasons for, or qualifications of, your chosen answer.

STATEMENT

1   The Medicines Act controls all aspects of dealing with medicines, including sales, advertising and wholesaling.

2   Pharmacists can choose the most suitable container for a medicine that they have made, without referring to the Medicines Act.

3   The Ministry of Agriculture, Fisheries and Food was generally responsible for veterinary medicines, but this function has been taken over by the recently formed Department for Environment, Food and Rural Affairs since publication of the seventh edition of *Pharmacy Law and Ethics*.

4   Those authorised by the Medicines Act to enforce the Act have no power to enter pharmacies and take samples of prescriptions that have already been dispensed.

5   The Medicines Act gives responsibility to those who enforce the Act – the inspectors – to maintain a register of pharmacies.

6   A pharmacist who prepares a cough medicine that has been made up according to a prescription from a doctor can do so. Any medicine which is made up by the pharmacist is still defined as a medicinal product.

What issues should I consider?

- What activities concerning medicines are controlled by the Medicines Act?
- Is the activity to be carried out by a community pharmacist controlled by the Medicines Act and should this be considered before proceeding?
- There are often additional legal and professional requirements to be considered too.

Where should I look in Pharmacy Law & Ethics?

Chapter 1 describes what the Medicines Act controls and how it is administered. Further questions will cover in detail how the Medicines Act affects the everyday activities of community pharmacists.

Answers and Explanations

2

1   **True**

The Medicines Act is wide-ranging and has many functions. The minister (or other official) responsible for administering and enforcing the Act takes advice from many experts, including the Medicines Commission.

2   **False**

The Act also controls the requirements for both the container and how it should be labelled for all medicines.

3   **True**

Again, panels of experts advise the Department.

4   **False**

The inspectors that enforce the Act – and these include the pharmaceutical inspectors who are responsible for the testing of medicinal products supplied from pharmacies – can take samples according to a set procedure.

5   **False**

The responsibility for maintaining the Register of Pharmacy Premises is given to the Royal Pharmaceutical Society of Great Britain (RPSGB).

6   False

A pharmacist may still prepare mixtures, and other pharmaceutical preparations such as creams, according to the directions given by the doctor who diagnoses the patient and prescribes for him or her. The practice is becoming much less common, due largely to the need for the quality of medicines to be controlled. A medicine made up in this way is called a magistral formula and is not a true medicinal product subject to all the requirements of the Medicines Act.

Question

3

Definitions used in the Medicines Act

The Medicines Act uses certain words and phrases to define exactly words that are often used in a vague way by the general public. For example, it does not use the word 'medicine' but includes the common interpretation of the term in the definition 'medicinal product'. Substances such as contraceptive pills that are not commonly described by the public as a medicine are also defined as a 'medicinal product'. (The absolutely correct term is a 'relevant medicinal product', but as the only type of medicinal product now available is now a relevant medicinal product, we will leave out the 'relevant'.)

Decide whether each of the following statements is true or false. You might also like to make a note of any reasons for, or qualifications of, your chosen answer.

STATEMENT

1   The *British Pharmacopoeia* (BP) is a 'specified publication'.

2   The *British National Formulary* (BNF) is a 'specified publication'.

3   Bendroflumethiazide is an appropriate non-proprietary name because this is the name that appears in the BP monograph.

4   Zantac is an example of a name given to a particular drug by the manufacturer to identify it as their product. It is commonly known as a proprietary (or 'brand') name, or, under the definitions of the Medicines Act, a Proprietary medicinal product.

5   The appropriate non-proprietary (approved) name for Zantac is ranitidine, which could be checked by looking in the BNF.

6   Condoms can be used for two medicinal purposes.

7   A condom is therefore a medicinal product because it is used for a medicinal purpose.

8   A mouthwash that is a medicinal product should be labelled 'for external use only'.

9   The appropriate quantitative particulars (the amount) of chlorphenamine (chlorpheniramine) in a Piriton tablet *could* be expressed as % w/w.

10   The strength of salbutamol in Ventolin syrup can be expressed as 2 mg/5 ml.

11   The level of activity or strength of Humulin S insulin can be expressed as 100 units per ml or 1000 units in a 10 ml vial.

12   The quantity of a homoeopathic medicine can be expressed as a dilution, for example, 6C.

13   All shampoos are cosmetics and are therefore exempt from the Medicines Act because they do not have a medicinal purpose.

14   Vitamin E cream can be classified as a cosmetic and is therefore exempt from the controls of the Medicines Act.

15   Vitamin preparations do not have to be sold from the area of a community pharmacy in which medicines are sold, as long as they are not labelled with an indication that they will cure a specific illness.

What issues should I consider?

■   The Medicines Act has its own very exact terminology, which you need to understand and be able to apply in order to appreciate some fundamental aspects of community pharmacy.

Where should I look in Pharmacy Law & Ethics?

Each Medicines Act definition is given on the first occasion it is used; as the terms appear in several chapters, the best way to find the one you want is to use the index. The entry you need is the one which refers to the 'meaning of'.

Answers and Explanations

3

1   True

A 'specified publication' is recognised as a reference source by the Medicines Act; the terminology is therefore standardised. Several much used reference books are not 'specified publications' and may contain information about substances not controlled by the Medicines Act.

2   False

The BNF is not in the list, and is therefore not a 'specified publication' – it falls into the category of a valuable reference source that is not recognised by the Medicines Act.

3   True

The appropriate non-proprietary name is the standard name by which the drug is known under the Medicines Act; if there is no monograph for the drug (an entry in the BP, for example), the drug can be known under the Medicines Act by its British Approved Name. There may be other names, or alternative spellings, which are not the 'official' name and not recognised under the Medicines Act but are given in reference sources such as the BNF. Bendroflumethiazide is a case in point; until very recently, its official name was Bendrofluazide, and most pharmacists will refer to it as such. If you have a look at a container of tablets you will see that the official BP name is given as either Bendroflumethiazide or bendrofluazide – very confusing. When the marketing authorisation for the product is renewed (which has to happen every five years at most), the new name will be used.

4   True

You will need to look in the BP to check that ranitidine is the correct appropriate non-proprietary name, of which Zantac is a preparation. The 'brand' names for a particular drug can be found in the BNF under 'preparations'. In the index, brand names are printed in italics.

5   False

The explanation is the same as for statement 1 above – but you cannot use the BNF to check, because it is not a 'specified publication' (statement 2).

6   True

From the definition of a medicinal purpose this is true, namely for (a) treating or preventing disease, for example, AIDS, and (c) for contraception.

7   False

Not necessarily! It is very hard to work out, but as it has no marketing authorisation number on the label it cannot be considered to be a medicinal product. Condoms are actually classified as medical devices and are not under the jurisdiction of the Medicines Act, but under consumer protection legislation.

8   True

The definition of external use for medicinal products (not all mouthwashes are) applies to the 'mucosa of the mouth'. Although the mouth may not seem to be 'external' the term 'for external use only' is the correct use under the Medicines Act, because the mouthwash does not get into the body and have a systemic effect.

9   False

The quantity in each dosage unit can be expressed in several ways; most often, for solid dosage forms like tablets, it is as a weight. The amount of the active ingredient can only be a percentage for pastilles and lozenges, which are used to treat infections of the throat. They have a localised rather than systemic action, so the amount of drug is not critical, as it is in a tablet where the drug acts on the whole body.

10   True

For liquid preparations that are intended for internal use, the amount of the drug present is expressed as weight per dosage unit volume – which for most liquid preparations is the 5 ml spoonful measured out from the bottle.

11   True

Certain products can be expressed as units of activity because they are assayed biologically and then standardised to that level of activity; the active ingredient cannot be produced as a definite concentration. Both the above statements are numerically correct.

12   True

Homoeopathic preparations can be expressed in terms of dilution of the unit preparation.

13   False

Shampoos that are used solely as a cosmetic are exempt. If a shampoo contains a substance that is a medicinal product because it is being used for a medicinal purpose – for example, treating a disease of the scalp such as psoriasis – then it is controlled by the Medicines Act and must have a marketing authorisation.

14   True

Vitamins are also exempt from the controls of the Medicines Act under certain circumstances, when they are defined as a food. The rules regarding their sale and labelling change considerably as a result.

15   True

If the vitamin is not sold with a recommendation that it can be used for a specific medicinal purpose, it is exempt from the Medicines Act and can be placed anywhere in the shop.

Question

The licensing system of the Medicines Act

The fundamental concept of the Medicines Act demands that every activity connected with a medicinal product is controlled by the terms of a licence, such as a wholesale dealer's licence or, in the case of a medicinal product, a marketing authorisation (previously known as a product licence).

Decide whether each of the following statements about licensing is true or false. You might also like to make a note of any reasons for, or qualifications of, your chosen answer.

STATEMENT

1   Every medicinal product available in the UK must have a marketing authorisation.

2   Every homoeopathic medicinal product available in the UK must have a marketing authorisation.

3   All marketing authorisation holders must have a manufacturer's licence to make their own product.

4   All marketing authorisation holders must have a wholesale dealer's licence to distribute their own product.

5   Every marketing authorisation that is issued is next reviewed five years later.

6   Every new dosage form of a medicinal product has to have a completely new marketing authorisation.

7   The main criteria for the granting of a marketing authorisation are the quality, safety and efficacy of the medicinal product.

8   A manufacturer's licence will be granted when the licensing authority is satisfied that the person supervising the manufacturing processes is suitably qualified.

9   The manufacturer of a product does not have to be the marketing authorisation holder.

10   One of the criteria for the granting of a wholesale dealer's licence is that arrangements are made for keeping suitable records.

11   A pharmacist does not need a marketing authorisation

to dispense an ointment that is made up for an individual patient against a doctor's prescription.

12 A pharmacist needs a manufacturer's licence to make small batches of medicine (e.g. Magnesium Trisilicate Mixture BP) for stock.

13 A pharmacist needs a marketing authorisation when making small quantities of a medicine whose formula he or she is responsible for and which is not advertised to the public.

14 A doctor can prescribe a medicinal product that does not have a marketing authorisation for an individual patient.

What issues should I consider?

- For each type of licence and for a marketing authorisation, there are criteria that have to be met before the licence or marketing authorisation is granted and the activity can proceed.
- There are also instances when certain people and activities are excluded from the need to have a licence.

Where should I look in Pharmacy Law & Ethics?

Chapter 2 describes the criteria for granting a licence and the exceptions to the rules for various practitioners and activities.

Answers and Explanations

1 **True**

The fundamental principle of the Medicines Act is the granting of an appropriate licence for any activity connected with medicines or – in the words of the Act – medicinal products. Until 1994, all medicinal products were granted a product licence once they had undergone rigorous testing. The term 'product licence' has now been replaced by the term 'marketing authorisation'.

2 **False**

As long as the homoeopathic medicinal product has been prepared using a manufacturing procedure described in the *European Pharmacopoeia* (or one used officially in an EU member state), it does not need a marketing authorisation, provided that a certificate of registration has been granted.

3 **True**

Anyone who manufactures (which includes any process carried out in the making) a medicinal product must have a manufacturer's licence; this includes the holder of the marketing authorisation.

4   False

No wholesale dealer's licence is needed by holders of a marketing authorisation to distribute their own product, so long as the medicinal product has not left the premises where it was made until it is sold.

5   False

A marketing authorisation is not always valid for five years. That is the maximum time for which a marketing authorisation can be valid, during which time it will be reviewed or can be varied; it can also be withdrawn so that it is no longer legal to sell the medicinal product.

6   False

Obviously a new pharmaceutical formulation must have a marketing authorisation, but it can be the subject of an abridged application if relevant data have been submitted previously.

7   True

Consideration is also given to factors such as the method of manufacture and quality control procedures, but the main criteria are the safety, quality and efficacy of the medicinal product.

8   False

The qualifications of the person(s) supervising the manufacturing of a medicinal product is only one of the criteria that will be considered; others include the premises and equipment.

9   True

The marketing authorisation holder can instruct a specialist manufacturer to make the medicinal product, provided that they have a manufacturer's licence.

10   True

There are other important criteria too that safeguard the distribution procedures for medicinal products.

11 True

This is one of the specific exemptions from the requirements of the Medicines Act for pharmacists, in recognition of their professional integrity and expertise to ensure that the result is a high quality product, even though it does not have the quality assurance associated with a mass-produced ointment.

12 False

This statement is false as long as the amount is small; a pharmacist making larger batches would have to have a manufacturer's licence.

13 False

However, if the medicinal product is advertised, then a marketing authorisation is needed.

14 True

The doctor could, for example, prescribe a product made abroad, i.e. not in a country that belongs to the EU, that does not have a UK marketing authorisation. This type of supply is commonly known as one for a 'named patient'.

Question

5

The controls on advertising medicinal products to the general public and to professionals

There are strict controls on the advertising of medicines to the general public, for obvious reasons. There are also restrictions on the promotion of medicinal products to practitioners.

Decide whether each of the following statements about the advertising of medicinal products is true or false. You might also like to make a note of any reasons for, or qualifications of, your chosen answer.

STATEMENT

1   POMs for human use cannot be advertised on television.

2   Pharmacy medicines (P) products cannot be advertised on television.

3   Eurax HC cream could be advertised in a newspaper.

4   All advertisements for P medicines must state the PL or marketing authorisation number of the product.

5   No advertisements are allowed for medicinal products that are applied to the eyes.

6   No advertisements for medicinal products are allowed that specifically target children.

7   A sedating antihistamine can be advertised as a sleeping tablet without breaking the law.

8   Advertisements for ibuprofen indicating that it can be used in treatment of dysmenorrhoea are allowed.

What issues should I consider?

- POMs for human use can never be advertised to the public; even P medicines, which can be purchased, cannot be advertised unless they comply with one of the exemptions to the rule that medicinal products cannot be advertised.

- No advertising of medicinal products for illnesses and conditions specified in the Medicines Act is allowed, even if they are legally available to the public.

- The wording and content of advertisements, both to the public and to professionals, are controlled by the Medicines Act.

- There are separate controls on the advertising of a pharmacy business and the services it provides; these are dealt with at Level 2.

Where should I look in Pharmacy Law & Ethics?

Chapter 3 on sales promotion describes the restrictions on advertising.

Answers and Explanations

5

1   **True**

Medicinal products for human use that are available only on prescription cannot be advertised to the public at all.

2   **False**

Medicinal products that are P medicines can, under certain circumstances, be advertised on television. The exact conditions include very specific requirements such as 'Always read the label' to be included.

3   **True**

Eurax HC is a P medicine licensed to treat mild to moderate eczema. As we have seen, P medicines can be advertised, providing that they are not to be used for a serious skin disorder. Although eczema can be very upsetting for the patient, it is not generally serious, so the product could be advertised.

4   False

This is a condition of an advertisement in a professional journal but is not required for advertisements directed at the general public, so does not apply to all advertisements.

5   False

We have already seen, in statement 3, that there are some exceptions to the general rule; no advertisements are allowed for serious disorders of the eye.

6   True

Some preparations taken by children are advertised, but the information is presented in a suitable manner for the parents, not their offspring.

7   True

The statement is true with the caveat that the preparation can only be advertised for the *temporary*, not chronic, relief of insomnia. As with so many advertisements, the wording is chosen extremely carefully to comply with the law, but also to imply more to a sometimes gullible public.

8   True

Dysmenorrhoea is more commonly known as period pains, and does not fall into any of the excluded categories for which advertisements are prohibited. In any advertisement, and by law on the leaflets provided to patients, the use of certain technical terms and medical conditions is to be avoided.

A further point to note is that ibuprofen is a POM drug that can only be sold as a P for certain conditions, dysmenorrhoea being one of them.

Question 6

The classification and sale of P and GSL products

Medicinal products are classified under the Medicines Act as either GSL (General Sale List) or POM. Any medicinal product that is not in one of these lists is automatically a P medicine. The legal classification has many implications as to how the medicinal product must be treated in the community pharmacy.

Decide whether each of the following statements is true or false. You might also like to make a note of any reasons for, or qualifications of, your chosen answer.

1   All medicinal products should normally be sold through pharmacies.

2   There is a definitive list of P medicines.

3   There are examples of aspirin and paracetamol packages that are legally classified as 'GSL' but must be treated in some respects as 'P' medicinal products.

4   Very specific restrictions apply to the pack sizes of certain preparations other than those containing aspirin and paracetamol if they are to be classified as GSL. For example, mepyramine maleate cream is a P, but a tube of cream that does not contain more than 2% of the active ingredient is a GSL.

5   There are some types of medicinal products that are never to be classified as GSL; they include all eye drops marketed and sold for human use.

6   GSL medicinal products for humans must be sold from a lockable shop, except when they are sold from a vending machine.

7   GSL products for veterinary use must be sold from a market stall.

8   A pack of 10 aspirin tablets could be sold from a vending machine in a pub.

9   A P medicine may not be sold when the pharmacist is checking prescriptions in the dispensary adjacent to the counter.

10   A large pack of 32 adult-strength paracetamol tablets can be sold when the pharmacist has gone upstairs for lunch.

What issues should I consider?

■ What are the regulations for selling GSL medicinal products?

■ What are the regulations for selling P medicinal products?

■ What do the regulations mean to a community pharmacist and the shop staff in terms of the legal requirements for selling medicines to the public?

■ There are separate professional requirements controlling supplies of medicines to the public, which are dealt with in Level 2 questions.

Where should I look in Pharmacy Law & Ethics?

Chapters 5 and 6 contain the information from the Medicines Act about the sale of GSL and P medicines; to find out more about how the law has interpreted some of the terms in the past, and what they mean to a community pharmacist, you will also need to read Chapters 21 and 26.

1   True

The basic principle of the Medicines Act is
products may only be sold from pharmacies.
classified as GSL or exempted from control in ₃
way (as foods and cosmetics, for example) are not sub,
the general rule, and can be sold from other shops.

2   False

A medicinal product can be classified as a POM or a GSL
medicine according to the Medicines Act. Any medicinal
product that is not on either of these two lists automatically
becomes a P medicine. There is no definitive list of P medicinal products, as explained in Chapter 5.

3   True

Certain drugs are only available for sale as 'normal' GSL
products when in small pack sizes. If the pack contains more
than a specified number it is sometimes referred to as a
'Pharmacy Only' (PO) medicine. Although legally classified
as GSL, the larger packs can only be sold under the personal
control (not supervision) of a pharmacist, which means that
they cannot be sold from other shops, unlike most GSL
medicinal products.

4   False

Mepyramine maleate is a P, but can be a GSL if very specific
restrictions are met. A strength of less than 2% is only one of
them; certain labelling conditions also have to be met.

5   True

A list of the types of medicinal products never to be on
general sale for humans includes eye drops.

6   False

Even a vending machine that contains medicinal products
must be situated in a lockable place so as to exclude the
public.

7   False

The conditions for the sale of GSL medicinal products
include specific exemptions from the requirements that apply
to GSLs sold for human use. They allow veterinary products
to be sold from a market stall or a van, but they do not have
to be sold in this way.

8   True

A pack of 10 aspirin tablets which are non-effervescent and where each tablet does not contain more than 300 mg are GSL. So long as the machine was situated in a location from which the public can be excluded, they could be sold from a vending machine in a pub.

9   False

The issue here is that of supervision and what it means in the practice situation. Put simply, the pharmacist must be in a position to intervene in the sale whenever a P medicine is sold by one of the pharmacy assistants. If the pharmacist is adjacent to the area where the medicines are sold, and therefore in a position to talk to the customer should it be thought necessary, the requirements are met and the P medicine may legally be sold.

10   False

Thirty-two paracetamol tablets are strictly speaking classified as a GSL, but the special conditions effectively limit the sale in the same way as that of a P medicinal product. That means the sale must be supervised and should not go ahead until the pharmacist returns. Following the same arguments as in the previous statement, it is impossible for the pharmacist to be in a position to intervene if he or she is not present.

Question

7

Labelling a 'P' medicinal product for sale

Any information about a medicinal product available for the public to buy may be forgotten if related orally, so there are very strict regulations to ensure that as much as possible of the necessary information is accessible to the purchaser in the form of printed instructions on the label. Although it is now usually the manufacturer who has the responsibility for ensuring that a medicinal product is labelled correctly, there are occasions where the pharmacist would be called upon to produce or check a sale label.

```
┌─────────────────────────────────────────────────────────────┐
│  ┌───┐                                                        │
│  │ P │          30 PIRITON 4 mg TABLETS                       │
│  └───┘            (Contain lactose BP)                        │
│                                                               │
│         ONE to be taken for hayfever THREE times a day        │
│                                                               │
│  Caution: May cause drowsiness; if affected do not drive or   │
│           operate machinery.                                  │
│           Avoid alcoholic drink.                              │
│  BN 0001            EXPIRY DATE JUNE 2005      MA 0000/6789    │
│                                                               │
│  ─────────────────────────────────────────────────────────   │
│  SOLD BY: HIGH STREET CHEMISTS      DATE OF SALE: 09 02 02     │
│           ANYTOWN                                             │
│           ANYWHERE    KEEP OUT OF REACH OF CHILDREN            │
│                                                               │
└─────────────────────────────────────────────────────────────┘
```

Study the 'label' carefully and decide which of the Medicines Act requirements have not been met for the situation described, using the following numbered guidelines.

1 There are several legal omissions; try to recognise them all.
2 There are three other omissions that may need to be included.
3 Two of the components are present but wrong; try to recognise and amend them.
4 Comment on any other aspects of the label, apart from the layout.
5 There are two things present that are *not* needed.

What issues should I consider?

- When producing and checking any label, it is vital to consider the use of the product, as the regulations vary; in this example the bottles of tablets are to be labelled ready for sale.
- All medicinal products that have been granted a marketing authorisation since 1 January 1994 are known as relevant medicinal products. When other products are relicensed, they will also become relevant medicinal products; there are specific labelling requirements for these products.
- There are general labelling requirements that apply to all medicinal products.
- There are extra labelling requirements for those medicinal products that are classified as P medicines and which can be sold to the public.

Where should I look in Pharmacy Law & Ethics? Chapter 14 describes the regulations for the identification of medicinal products and their packaging; check that you are referring to the section on the labelling for sale of relevant medicinal products, and also the extra information required for those that are P medicines.

Answers and Explanations

7

Before considering the example given in detail, the general regulations that apply to all labels for relevant medicinal products should be considered. The regulations state that all labels must be legible, comprehensible, indelible and in English.

The specific details included are those of the standard labelling requirements; the numbers in brackets refer to the appropriate standard requirements. As chlorphenamine (chlorpheniramine) is legally classified as a P medicine, the extra requirements also apply.

1   The legal omissions are:

(a)   The active ingredients are not stated qualitatively and quantitatively using the 'common name' as defined by the Medicines Act, i.e. 'Each tablet contains chlorpheniramine B.P. 4 mg' (2).

(b)   The name and address of the holder of the marketing authorisation must be given (11).

(c)   As the name of the product is an invented (proprietary) name, the common name must follow it (1).

2   The three other omissions that *may* need to be included are:

(a)   Special precautions for storage (9).

(b)   Special precautions for the disposal of unused tablets (10).

(c)   Any special warning if this is necessary for the medicinal product (7), which would be a condition of the marketing authorisation. For example, it could be a condition of the marketing authorisation that an aspirin preparation is labelled 'Not to be taken by children under 12'.

3   The necessary amendments are:

(a)   When sedating antihistamines such as chlorphenamine (chlorpheniramine) are sold, the label must include the extra/statutory warning number 5, to alert the purchaser to the likely adverse effect. On the label for a dispensed product, the same information is conveyed to the patient by means of a strongly recommended cautionary label. The wording is exactly the same, except that the word 'caution' is used on a dispensed label and 'warning' on the one for sale. The whole warning phrase should be contained in a rectangle in which there is no other matter.

(b)   As already mentioned, the name and address of the marketing authority holder, not the shop, must be given on the label.

4   Other comments could well be:

•   The dose is incomplete and could be extended to include the information in the BNF; full information about the product and the terms of its marketing authority would be found in the Summary of Product Characteristics. Point 14 states that, for self-medication, instructions must be given. It is generally accepted that these would be as detailed as practicable, but would refer to 'one tablet' rather than 4 mg, for example.

•   The indication is also incomplete; chlorphenamine (chlorpheniramine) can be sold for several other allergic conditions – again you would need to consult the marketing authorisation for details of exactly what it can be sold for.

•   Points 3, 4, 5, 6 and 8 are covered satisfactorily.

5   The two things present that are *not* needed are:

(a)   the date of sale;

(b)   the name and address of the shop (as already mentioned).

Question 8

Labelling a dispensed medicine

A medicinal product that is supplied to a particular patient on prescription at the request of a practitioner is labelled less stringently than for sales as the instructions apply to an individual. The requirements are still determined by the Medicines Act, but additional recommendations are made by the RPSGB.

Decide whether each of the following statements is true or false. You might also like to make a note of any reasons for, or qualifications of, your chosen answer.

STATEMENT   1   The name and address of the pharmacy that supplies the medicine must be on the label.

2   If the prescriber does not write any dose or directions on the prescription, the pharmacist will add some, using the BNF to guide him.

3   A patient who does not speak or understand English asks for the instructions on the prescription to be put on the label in their own language. A counter assistant offers to translate for you; as they are fluent in the language and you know it will be correct, the label will meet the requirements of the Medicines Act.

4   If a computer-generated label misses off the words 'Keep out of the reach of children' because it has not been lined up properly, it will not matter if the medicine is for a person who does not have children living in the house.

Where should I look in Pharmacy Law & Ethics?   Chapter 14 describes the regulations for the identification of medicinal products and their packaging; check that you are referring to the section on the labelling of relevant dispensed medicinal products.

Answers and Explanations

8

1   **True**

The name of the pharmacy counts as 'the name of the person who sells or supplies' the medication.

2   **False**

Although it is not good practice for the doctor to omit to tell the patient in writing what may have been passed on verbally (the patient will probably forget), the pharmacist must not add their own directions. It would be preferable to contact the prescriber by telephone and confirm what was intended, then they can be added according to the conversation. If the instructions to the patient were considered to be inappropriate, and the prescriber could not be contacted, then the pharmacist might use his professional judgement and advise the patient accordingly.

3   **False**

Although the standard labelling requirements do not apply to dispensed medicines, the general labelling provisions do. The label must be in English and you can add one or more other languages, provided that the same particulars appear in all the languages used.

4   False

These words, or something very similar, have to be on every label for dispensed and sale labels as a legal requirement of the Medicines Act, regardless of the circumstances.

Question 9

The labelling of medicines for sale that are exempt from POM and controlled drug controls by limitations as to maximum strength, dose and form

Pholcodine is one of the six controlled drugs that can be exempted from the regulations that restrict the sale of such preparations, provided that certain conditions are met. Depending on the limitations on the strength and/or the dose, the preparation can be classified as a POM or a P medicine. For each of the controlled drugs, the conditions under which they can be sold are different; when any of the drugs meets the requirements for being sold as a P medicine, there are additional labelling requirements.

Pholcodine Linctus BP is labelled with the words 'Warning. Do not exceed the stated dose'.

STATEMENT

1   Explain exactly why this wording must be on the Pholcodine Linctus.

2   A new 'Pholcodine Linctus' is made up by a pharmacist for his customers. It contains 20 mg/5 ml Pholcodine HCl and is sold to 'soothe the throat and chest'. What is the maximum volume that the pharmacist can recommend to be taken as a dose when the preparation is sold?

3   The new preparation is very popular with the pharmacist's customers, and he decides to get it made on a large scale and sell it more widely, advertising the preparation in the local press. Briefly describe three restrictions that the Medicines Act would place on these proposals.

What issues should I consider?

■   For each of the six controlled drugs, the limitations as to the maximum strength, the maximum dose and the pharmaceutical form are different.

■   If any of the drugs are to be sold, the conditions for sale for that drug must be met, otherwise the sale will be illegal.

■   All the controlled drugs sold as P medicines under these exemptions must be labelled according to the statutory requirements in addition to the normal labelling of P medicines for sale.

Where should I look in Pharmacy Law & Ethics?   Chapter 7 describes the six drugs in question and the limitations on their strength, dose and form that have to be met before they can be sold.

Answers and Explanations

1   Pholcodine is a controlled drug, and therefore also a POM; it can only be sold as a P if the preparation meets the following conditions:

- The strength does not exceed the allowable maximum of 1.5 % pholcodine.
- The stated dose does not exceed the allowable maximum of 20 mg.
  Pholcodine Linctus BP contains 5 mg/5 ml pholcodine. It therefore fulfils the first condition as the strength is only 0.1 %. In order to comply with the second condition above, the stated dose must be a volume that would give a dose of less than 20 mg. For this preparation, the stated dose must be fewer than four 5-ml spoonfuls, or the maximum dose (md) of 20 mg will be exceeded. Obviously, a customer who bought the preparation and took more than the stated dose might exceed the dose that can be bought legally, hence the requirement under the P labelling regulations for all such preparations to be labelled with the words 'Warning. Do not exceed the stated dose'.

2   Pholcodine is only a P medicine when the maximum dose is 20 mg (and the maximum strength 1.5%). Consequently, if the label instructs the patient to take more than 5 ml, the dose of pholcodine would exceed that which can legally be sold.

3   The restrictions that the Medicines Act would impose are as follows:

- If the preparation is advertised to the public, it must have a marketing authorisation.
- If the preparation is made on a large scale, the manufacturer, even if it is a pharmacist, must have a manufacturer's licence.
- If the preparation is advertised, it must not refer to the treatment of any serious respiratory diseases.

The above hypothetical example illustrates how the requirements of the Medicines Act will act to control the supply of an inappropriate medication and protect the public.

Question 10

A labelling summary

The labelling requirements for medicinal products that are supplied to the public alter to meet the needs of the situation. To summarise the requirements, copy out the table below and enter *one* legally necessary labelling requirement – for example, 'the quantity of dosage units' – in *each* of the boxes.

Each box in the table must have a different piece of information in it!

Hint: think carefully about which information could be entered in more than one box and which is specific to a particular situation. Enter the latter type first, then complete the other boxes (in pencil) with the pieces of information that can go in more than one box.

What issues should I consider?

- You will need to remind yourself of all the labelling regulations that you have covered so far – for both GSL medicines and P medicines – for sale and for dispensing.
- You will need to look up the exact legal category of each of the three drugs.

		Situation in which drug is supplied		
Drug	Exact Legal classification	Sale to member of the public	Dispensed on an NHS prescription	Prepacked in the pharmacy from a large pack, ready for dispensing
Drug 1: 20 paracetamol tablets 500 mg				
Drug 2: 56 aspirin tablets 300 mg dispersible				
Drug 3: Codeine linctus BP 100 ml				
Any drug	No answer			

Where should I look in Pharmacy Law & Ethics?

In order to find the exact legal category of each drug, you will need to consult *Medicines Ethics and Practice: a Guide for Pharmacists*. Use the most recent version you can. All the information about labelling has been covered in Questions 7, 8 and 9; you can also consult Chapter 14 again, but try to use the question to test yourself first.

Answers and Explanations

10

This is a suggestion of how the boxes might look, as some pieces of information are interchangeable. Take care not to use the same legal requirement more than once!

	Situation in which drug is supplied			
Drug	*Exact Legal classification*	*Sale to member of the public*	*Dispensed on an NHS prescription*	*Prepacked in the pharmacy from a large pack, ready for dispensing*
Drug 1: 20 paracetamol tablets 500 mg	GSL but treated as a P	Do not exceed stated dose	Do not take more than two at any one time: do not take more than eight in 24 hours	Expiry date
Drug 2: 56 aspirin tablets 300 mg dispersible	GSL but treated as a P	Self-medication instructions, i.e. dose	Name of the patient	Storage requirements
Drug 3: Codeine linctus BP 100 ml	CD Inv P	The amount of codeine in each 5-ml spoonful	The name and address of the seller/ supplier	Batch number
Any drug	No answer	The number of tablets in the container	Keep out of reach of children	Name of the drug

Question

11

The Medicines Act requirements for POM supplies

This question deals with the legal requirements for prescriptions for POMs. Decide whether each of the following statements is true or false. You might also like to make a note of any reasons for, or qualifications of, your chosen answer.

STATEMENT

1 The prescription must be completely hand-written by the doctor.
2 The prescription is not valid if presented for dispensing on the day before the date on the prescription.
3 The prescription is valid for six months from the date on the prescription.
4 The prescription can be valid even if there is no exact quantity of tablets stated on the prescription.
5 The name of the drug on the prescription is furosemide, which is an appropriate non-proprietary name.
6 Any directions on the prescription are not legally necessary.
7 The prescription can be repeated at a later date.
8 It is necessary to check that the signature is genuine – that it is the signature of a doctor registered in the UK as a general medical practitioner.
9 If the prescription were for a child under 12, the child's age would have to be stated in the box provided.
10 A prescription issued by a vet will always have to indicate that the treatment is for an animal under his or her care.

What issues are involved?

■ The Medicines Act has specific requirements that must be met when a POM is prescribed; this question tests your understanding of those legal requirements using an NHS prescription as an example.

Where should I look in Pharmacy Law & Ethics?

Chapter 7 describes the Medicines Act requirements for POMs.

Answers and Explanations

11

1 False

As long as the prescription is written in ink or some other 'indelible' form, e.g. typed or computer generated, it does not matter if it was filled in by someone other than the doctor, for example, a receptionist. In Question 17 you will find examples of prescription types that do have to be hand-written by the prescriber.

2 True

The appropriate date is taken to be the date on the prescription, and this is the earliest date on which it can be dispensed.

3 True

As above.

4   True

If all the legal requirements – signature and address of practitioner, appropriate date and type of practitioner – are present, it's valid. If the prescription had been for a child under 12, the age would also have to be stated. The quantity is not a legal requirement, and can be indicated as the number of days treatment to be given by writing on the NHS form in the box provided. This information, together with the dose and frequency of administration, enable the quantity to be dispensed to be calculated.

5   True

As already explained in Question 3, an appropriate non-proprietary name would need to be checked in a specified publication. The BNF and *Martindale* are not in this category, but use them to check alternative forms of the name. Use the BP monograph in this case.

6   True

There is no legal requirement for the prescriber to include directions. As a pharmacist, you should check that any directions given are appropriate to the patient and his or her condition, and applicable to the medication. You should also ensure that the patient knows how to take the medication, and check with the doctor if in any doubt.

7   False

This is not a 'repeatable prescription' but a 'health' (NHS) prescription and may not be repeated.

8   True

Pharmacists must always check that a prescription is not forged. Even if a pharmacist has taken all reasonable steps, i.e. checked as far as possible that a prescription is genuine, dispensing a forged prescription is unlawful. However, in this case, although the pharmacist has committed a legal offence, there *may* be a defence for his or her actions. This type of situation is discussed further at Level 2.

9   True

If the prescription is for a child under 12, it is a legal requirement of the Medicines Act that the child's age is stated. On NHS forms, a box for the age to be included is provided.

10   True

The requirement is normally printed on the prescription.

Question 12

The wholesale supply of POMs

The following statements are concerned with the meaning of the term 'wholesale supply' and the conditions under which a wholesale dealer's licence is required.

Complete the following sentences by inserting a word in each space.

1. A wholesale supply of a POM is a supply to someone who is going to use it in connection with his or her ...., ... or ....

2. A wholesale dealer's licence is required if the person to whom the POM is being supplied is then going to .... or .... the medicinal product to others on a large scale.

3. A wholesale dealer's licence is required if the person to whom the POM is being .... is then going to supply the medicinal product to others; however, ... /........ / .... do not need a wholesale dealer's licence to administer a medicinal product to their patients or to the patients of another .... who has asked them to do so.

4. A wholesale dealer's licence is not required for:

   (a) Transporting of a medicinal product by the .... holder.

   (b) A .... when selling his or her own products.

   (c) A .... who supplies other professionals with medicinal products very occasionally.

   (d) A .... who distributes medicinal products to others in a small group of pharmacies.

5. It is good practice to obtain a .... for the wholesale supply of POM medicinal products; however, it is not a legal requirement, so long as a record is made in the prescription-only register.

What issues should I consider?

- Think about the criteria that make a sale a wholesale supply rather than a normal retail sale.
- Consider also the criteria that must be met before a wholesale dealer's licence is granted.

Where should I look in Pharmacy Law & Ethics? You will need to read the definition of a wholesale supply and to find the criteria for the granting of a wholesale dealer's licence. Wholesale supplies are covered in Chapter 9.

Answers and Explanations

12

The complete sentence is given, with the words that you should have inserted in *italics*.

1   A wholesale supply of a POM is a supply to someone who is going to use it in connection with his or her *trade*, *business* or *profession*.

2   A wholesale dealer's licence is required if the person to whom the POM is being supplied is then going to *sell* or *supply* the medicinal product to others on a large scale.

3   A wholesale dealer's licence is required if the person to whom the POM is being *supplied* is then going to supply the medicinal product to others; however, *doctors/vets/dentists* do not need a wholesale dealer's licence to administer a medicinal product to their patients, or to the patients of another *practitioner* who has asked them to do so.

4   A wholesale dealer's licence is not required for:

(a)   Transporting a medicinal product by the *marketing authorisation* holder.

(b)   A *manufacturer* when selling his or her own products.

(c)   A *pharmacist* who supplies other professionals with medicinal products very occasionally.

(d)   A *pharmacist* who distributes medicinal products to others in a small group of pharmacies.

5   It is good practice to obtain a *signed order* for the wholesale supply of POM medicinal products; however, it is not a legal requirement, so long as a record is made in the prescription-only register.

Question

13

An emergency supply of a POM at the request of a patient

Pharmacists have the facility under the Medicines Act to supply, at their discretion, certain POM medicinal products to the public without a prescription, in an emergency. However, there are legal (and ethical) restrictions to be considered before such a supply can be made, which are detailed in this question.

Consider the following scenario. A regular customer enters the shop late on Saturday afternoon and asks to speak to the pharmacist. She asks to 'borrow' some of her tablets as she has run out. Your patient medication record (PMR) confirms that she takes Atenolol tablets, 50 mg each morning. Are you able to give her some as an 'emergency supply at the request of a patient'?

For each of the legal requirements that apply if the supply is to be made – which are listed below – indicate whether or not the condition is fulfilled in the scenario above. If the facts are not given, explain what extra information is needed, and how you would obtain it.

1   The pharmacist has interviewed the patient and determined:

(a)   there is an immediate need for the medication and it is impracticable in the circumstances to obtain a prescription;

(b)   the treatment has been prescribed before for the person requesting it;

(c)   the dose is known and appropriate.

2   With certain exceptions, no more than five days' supply can be given.

3   An entry is made in the prescription-only register with the details listed. (The prescription-only register is the register kept for the supply of medicines other than those on NHS prescriptions. It usually consists of a large book kept in the dispensary, in which 'private' prescription details are recorded.)

4   A label is issued with all the details listed.

5   The POM is not a controlled drug in Schedule 2 or 3 or a drug on a specified list.

What issues should I consider?

The conditions that legally have to be met before an emergency supply of a POM at the request of a patient is made consist of:

■   a series of questions that must be answered satisfactorily by the patient;

■   records that have to be kept;

■   labelling regulations that must be adhered to;

■   limitations on the amount that can be supplied.

Where should I look in Pharmacy Law & Ethics?

Consider each of the legal requirements for emergency supplies at the request of a patient in Chapter 7 and decide if the information is sufficient to meet the requirements or if other criteria must be met and, if so, how this would be done.

Answers and Explanations

13

1   Yes. The patient asked to speak to the pharmacist.

(a)   The patient has run out of tablets, but this alone is not sufficient to merit an emergency supply. She must have a condition that needs immediate or continuous treatment, which is not obvious from the scenario. You could *either* ask her exactly why she needs them or find out from the PMR for what condition she takes the Atenolol tablets. In this instance, it is for hypertension. Another factor to assist you in your decision to supply in this instance is the use of cautionary label 8: 'Do not stop taking this medicine except on your doctor's advice'. It is Saturday afternoon, so it is very unlikely that the doctor is available, but efforts must be made to obtain a prescription or at least talk to a doctor who can prescribe by phone. Ring the surgery to be certain – try to get a prescription.

(b)   The dosage details are on the PMR, and you know that she takes the medication for hypertension. The BNF will tell you that the dose is appropriate, so the legal requirement is met. If a PMR record is not available, the patient must be questioned as to the medication taken, when it was last prescribed, the dose taken and the frequency.

2   There are a few exceptions to the five-day maximum supply rule, for packages such as inhalers that cannot be split. As she can get a new prescription on Monday giving her a maximum of five days' supply will not be a problem.

3   So long as the exact details of why the supply is necessary have been established, all the details listed are known and the entry can be made. Note that the reason and the 'nature of the emergency' must be recorded. It is not sufficient to write 'run out of tablets', for example. A reason must also be given as to why this is deemed to be a sufficient emergency to warrant a supply without having a prescription.

4   Again the label should not be a problem. Ideally, a record of the supply should be added to her PMR, along with the fact that an emergency supply has been

made. The words 'Emergency Supply' must be on the label.

5   Atenolol is not a controlled drug, and a supply is allowed. If the request is for an unusual drug, the list and legal status must be checked before the possibility of making such a supply is discussed.

In this question we have considered the legal points that must be covered before a simple emergency supply at the request of a patient can be made. In Question 9 at Level 2 the further ethical issues that should be considered are examined. Finally, at Level 3, the more difficult professional decisions that sometimes have to be made are discussed in depth.

Question

14

An emergency supply at the request of a doctor

Instead of contacting you, suppose the patient in Question 13 manages to speak to her doctor, who rings you to request an emergency supply of her medication. Consider the following questions regarding the differences and similarities in the supply.

1   Can the receptionist ring you or does it have to be the doctor?
2   Can the doctor prescribe a new drug or must it be one the patient has had before?
3   Can the doctor prescribe more than five days' supply?
4   Is there a time limit as to when the doctor must send you the prescription?
5   Can a doctor who is very busy give all his or her prescriptions by telephone?
6   Do the words 'Emergency Supply' need to be on the label?
7   Do any records need to be made?
8   Can other practitioners request an emergency supply?
9   How could a dentist obtain a supply of antibiotics to supply to a patient without supplying you with a prescription?
10 Can a doctor request an emergency supply of pheno-barbital, even though it is a controlled drug?

What issues should I consider?

■   What conditions legally have to be met before an emergency supply at the request of a doctor can be made, including the records that have to be kept?

Where should I look in Pharmacy Law & Ethics?

An emergency supply at the request of a doctor is covered in Chapter 7.

Answers and Explanations

14

1   The pharmacist must be satisfied that the sale or supply has been requested by a doctor – so you need to speak to him or her. If you do not know the doctor, you should check it was a UK-registered doctor that you spoke to. Note that emergency supplies from other practitioners are not covered in the Medicines Act and are therefore illegal.

2   So long as it is not a controlled drug in Schedule 2 or 3, any medication can be supplied, whether or not the patient has had it before.

3   Yes – there is no limit specified.

4   Yes – the law says that the doctor 'has undertaken to furnish the person lawfully conducting the retail pharmacy business with a prescription within 72 hours' of the telephone request. In this sense, the word 'furnish' means supply or provide, so the doctor has three days in which to send the prescription.

5   No – the facility is for use ' by reason of an emergency'. For example, a doctor who had gone on an urgent house call without a prescription pad would be 'unable to furnish a prescription immediately'.

6   No – to the patient, it is a normal supply that has been given by telephone in the first instance, instead of by a written prescription.

7   Yes, a detailed record needs to be made; this is the only occasion when a record of an NHS transaction is made in the prescription-only register. In addition to the normal details needed for a private prescription, a space must be left to enter the date on the prescription and the name of the doctor who signed it, and the date on which it arrives.

8   No – the facility is strictly for an emergency supply made at the request of a *doctor*.

9   You could supply the dentist directly as a wholesale supply.

10   Yes, an exception to the rule that no controlled drugs in Schedules 2 and 3 may be supplied is made specifically for this condition. Anyone else who is prescribed phenobarbital may not have an emergency supply, even if a doctor requests it.

Question 15

The general requirements of the Misuse of Drugs Act

The drugs controlled under the Misuse of Drugs Act 1971 are classified into five Schedules under the Misuse of Drugs Regulations 1985. Each Schedule has different levels of control that a pharmacist has to adhere to. Schedule 1 does not concern community pharmacists, as it deals with the hallucinogens and other drugs which, although they are commonly misused, are not available as medicinal products. For each of the Schedules 2–5 inclusive (commonly known by the

	Schedule 2 (CD POM)	Schedule 3 (CD No Reg POM)	Schedule 4 Part I (CD Anab POM)	Schedule 4 Part II (CD Benz POM)	Schedule 5 (CD Inv P or POM)
1 Should a CD register entry be made when drugs are received?					
2 Should a CD register entry be made when drugs are supplied?					
3 Is an 'emergency supply at request of patient' allowed?					
4 Is a requisition legally needed for a wholesale supply?					
5 Does the destruction of out-of-date stock need to be supervised (assuming that environmental regulations are not being contravened)?					
6 Is it necessary to use 'safe custody', i.e. the CD cupboard, for storage?					
7 Should the invoice be retained by the community pharmacist for two years?					

titles in brackets at the top of each column in the table
above), compare the controls that apply. In answering the
questions for each Schedule, remember that every controlled
drug (except those that are a 'P' medicine) is also a POM.
Include any exceptions to the general rule in your answers.

*What
issues
should I
consider?*

■ Think about the controls on the activities listed in the
table above that apply to each schedule (in ordinary
language, the group) of controlled drugs.

*Where should
I look in
Pharmacy
Law & Ethics?*

The regimes of control are described in Chapter 16.

Answers and Explanations 15	Schedule 2 (CD POM)	Schedule 3 (CD No Reg POM)	Schedule 4 Part I (CD Anab POM)	Schedule 4 Part II (CD Benz POM)	Schedule 5 (CD Inv P or POM)
1 Should a CD register entry be made when drugs are received?	Yes	No	No	No	No
2 Should a CD register entry be made when drugs are supplied?	Yes	No	No	No	No
3 Is an 'emergency supply at request of patient' allowed?	No	No*	Yes	Yes	Yes – but can sell those that are P medicines†
4 Is a requisition legally needed for a wholesale supply?	Yes	Yes	No	No	No
5 Does the destruction of out-of-date stock need to be supervised (assuming that environmental regulations are not being contravened)?	Yes	No	No	No	No

	Schedule 2 (CD POM)	Schedule 3 (CD No Reg POM)	Schedule 4 Part I (CD Anab POM)	Schedule 4 Part II (CD Benz POM)	Schedule 5 (CD Inv P or POM)
6 Is it necessary to use 'safe custody', i.e. the CD cupboard, for storage?	Yes, except seco-barbital	No‡	No	No	No
7 Should the invoice be retained by the community pharmacist for two years?	No (CD entry is kept for two years)	Yes	No	No	Yes

* Except for the treatment of epileptics with phenobarbitone.
† See Question 9 concerning the classification of controlled drugs that can be exempted from POM control because of the md, ms and form of the preparation.
‡ Preparations of temazepam, buprenorphine and diethylpropion must be stored in the CD cupboard.

Question 16

The authority to possess and supply under the Misuse of Drugs Act

Certain groups of people, by nature of their profession, are authorised to possess and supply specified controlled drugs. Individuals such as patients are authorised to possess only when they have received a valid prescription.

Decide whether or not the following scenarios breach the restrictions imposed by the Misuse of Drugs Act regarding the possession and supply of controlled drugs.

1   A pharmacist delivering Methadone Linctus to a patient who had presented an NHS prescription.

2   A taxi driver collecting Temgesic injections (issued on an NHS prescription) for someone who is housebound.

3   A pharmacy assistant collecting phenobarbital tablets 30 mg from another pharmacy.

4   A police constable taking some LSD seized in a raid back to the police station.

5   A vet who urgently requires morphine injections but who cannot supply the written order (requisition) until the next day.

6   A Customs and Excise officer smoking cannabis at a party.

7   A doctor who orders Diconal tablets on a private prescription for himself.

8   A midwife who destroys pethidine injections that are past their expiry date.

9   An epileptic who requests an emergency supply of phenobarbital.

What issues should I consider?

- Is the person authorised to possess all or any controlled drugs as a member of a particular profession?
- Is the person authorised to possess all or any controlled drugs as an individual in the course of his or her work?
- In the case of a supply, is the person authorised to supply controlled drugs and, if so, which ones?
- What penalties might be imposed if a pharmacist possesses controlled drugs other than in the course of business activities?

Where should I look in Pharmacy Law & Ethics?

The different classes of people that are authorised to possess and supply are listed, together with the controlled drug schedule(s) that they are authorised to possess and/or supply and any other conditions that must be met, in Chapter 16.

Answers and Explanations

16

1   A pharmacist is authorised to possess and supply Schedule 2, 3, 4 and 5 controlled drugs when lawfully conducting a retail pharmacy business, and the patient is authorised to possess the drug by virtue of holding an NHS prescription. A pharmacist who is transporting the supply from his or her place of business to the patient is acting legally because delivering prescriptions is part of the professional services that pharmacists can offer as part of their business.

2   Again, the patient is authorised to possess. The taxi driver is in business as a carrier and is authorised to possess the supply to transport it directly from the shop to the patient.

3   When one pharmacist supplies another pharmacy, the transaction is a wholesale supply, as described in Chapter 9. The pharmacy assistant would therefore need to have a 'messenger's authority' issued by the purchasing pharmacist in order to be legally in possession of the controlled drug.

4   Police constables acting in the course of their duty, as this one obviously is, are authorised to possess all controlled drugs including the hallucinogenic Schedule 1 drug LSD.

5   Under the Misuse of Drugs Act it is illegal for a practitioner to issue a prescription, and for a pharmacist to dispense it and supply the controlled drug, unless a valid prescription (Question 17) is in the possession of the pharmacist. However, a wholesale supply can legally be made to a practitioner – including a vet – on the understanding that the requisition (the written order) is provided within 24 hours.

6   Although an officer of Customs and Excise is authorised to possess all classes of controlled drug when acting in the course of his duty, possession at a party is clearly not in the line of duty and is illegal.

7   Although a doctor is, of course, a practitioner and allowed to possess and supply all controlled drugs except those in Schedule 1, the Home Office specifically states that it regards possession by a doctor on the strength of a prescription issued for him or herself as illegal.

8   Midwives are authorised to possess and administer pethidine when legally supplied to her on a 'Midwives Supply order', which means that the supply has been authorised by the 'appropriate medical officer'. If the supply is not used, it must be surrendered to that person or to the person who supplied it.

9   In the regulations concerning 'emergency supplies,' controlled drugs in Schedules 2 and 3 are specifically excluded, with the exception of phenobarbitone for an epileptic patient. The supply and possession is therefore legal, providing that the normal conditions for an emergency supply have been met.

Another issue to consider, although it is not included in the questions, is the position of a pharmacist possessing a controlled drug when not at work, and not delivering to a customer. Examples would be the possession of a Schedule 1 drug (which pharmacists are never authorised to possess) or a Schedule 2 drug (which they are authorised to possess and supply only in the course of their business) for recreational use.

In either of these instances, a pharmacist is as liable to be arrested and penalised as any other member of the public would be. The penalties for unauthorised possession are divided into three classes according to the drug in question, as described in Appendix 10. For a pharmacist, however, the penalties are likely to be even more severe, as a criminal offence, once proven, would be followed up by the RPSGB and an appearance in front of the Statutory Committee could lead to the loss of the right to practice.

Question

17

Prescription requirements for controlled drugs

We have already seen in Question 15 that controlled drugs are classified into five Schedules, but that community pharmacists are not concerned with those in Schedule 1. For each of the Schedules 2–5 inclusive (commonly known by the titles in brackets at the top of each column in the table below), compare the controls that apply to prescriptions; include any exceptions to the general rule in your answers.

	Schedule 2 (CD POM)	Schedule 3 (CD No Reg POM)	Schedule 4 Part I (CD Anab POM)	Schedule 4 Part II (CD Benz POM)	Schedule 5 (CD Inv P or POM)
1 All details need to be hand-written by the prescriber?					
2 Quantity to be written in words and figures?					
3 Pharmaceutical 'Form' to be included?					
4 Dose and frequency to be stated?					
5 Valid for . . . (length of time)?					
6 Is the supply repeatable if private?					
7 Can they be dated by computer?					
8 Is there a need to check signature of the doctor?					
9 Is there a need to check that the doctor is registered in the UK?					

What issues should I consider?

■ You will need to think carefully about the prescription requirements for the different schedules of controlled drugs.

Where should I look in Pharmacy Law & Ethics?

The prescription requirements for the different controlled drugs are described in Chapter 16.

Answers and Explanations *17*	Schedule 2 (CD POM)	Schedule 3 (CD No Reg POM)	Schedule 4 Part I (CD Anab POM)	Schedule 4 Part II (CD Benz POM)	Schedule 5 (CD Inv P or POM)
1 All details need to be hand-written by the prescriber?	Yes	Yes*	No	No	No
2 Quantity to be written in words and figures?	Yes	Yes†	No	No	No
3 Pharmaceutical 'Form' to be included?	Yes	Yes†	No	No	No
4 Dose and frequency to be stated?	Yes	Yes†	No	No	No
5 Valid for . . . (length of time)?	13 weeks	13 weeks	6 months	6 months	6 months (if POM)‡
6 Is the supply repeatable if private?	No	No	Yes	Yes	Yes
7 Can they be dated by computer?	No	No	Yes	Yes	Yes
8 Is there a need to check signature of the doctor?	Yes	Yes	Yes	Yes	'No' if P
9 Is there a need to check that the doctor is registered in the UK?	Yes	Yes	Yes	Yes	'No' if P

* Not for phenobarbital or temazepam.
† Not for temazepam.
‡ See Question 9 concerning the classification of controlled drugs that can be exempted from POM control because of the md, ms and form of the preparation.

Question
18

The supply of controlled drugs other than on a prescription

A local doctor whom you know well, Dr Cureall, needs an urgent supply of pethidine ampoules delivered to his surgery. He sends his receptionist, Mrs Deacon, to collect them. You will need to decide first of all whether or not the supply is legally possible. As a part of that decision, you will need to consider all the types of supply to a doctor that can take place, and the controls that would apply, in order to answer the questions that will guide you to the answer.

You may also find it helpful to refer to Question 16 concerning the possession of controlled drugs.

1   The doctor wants a supply of a controlled drug to be made directly to him. What type of supply is therefore being requested?

2   Under what conditions does the doctor become exempt from the restrictions on the retail sale of medicinal products?

3   The doctor is automatically authorised to possess the controlled drug because he is a practitioner; he can legally possess it to use on his patients. Is his receptionist, Mrs Deacon, *automatically* authorised to possess the controlled drug in these circumstances?

4

(a)   What document(s), if any, need to be made available to you before you can legally supply the drug to Dr Cureall?

(b)   Can the supply be made via Mrs Deacon? Or does the doctor have to collect them from you in person?

What issues should I consider?

■   The first one to consider is the type of supply that is being requested, and then whether or not it can legally be made via a third party.

■   If you have decided that it is a supply that can legally be made, you next need to consider the conditions that apply, bearing in mind the legal classification of the drug being requested.

■   Finally, you need to think carefully about the records that need to be kept and how you will deal with any necessary paperwork.

Where should I look in Pharmacy Law & Ethics?

It has already been suggested that you need to remind yourself of who can legally be authorised to possess controlled drugs automatically, and the conditions under which carriers and intermediaries can be authorised temporarily, by looking again at Question 16. You will also need to consider the special circumstances for the supply of a controlled drug, and also the method of recording such a transaction.

When Mrs Deacon arrives at your pharmacy, she hands over two documents. Study them carefully and then answer the following additional questions.

Document 1

> THE SURGERY
> 17 MAIN RD
> ANYTOWN
> TODAY'S DATE
>
> Please supply me with 2 pethidine ampoules (100 mg) for use in the surgery
>
> (Signed by) Dr Cureall
> Dr S L Cureall MB ChB

Document 2

> Please allow my receptionist Mrs Deacon to collect 2 pethidine ampoules (100 mg)
>
> (Signed by) Dr Cureall
> Dr S L Cureall MB ChB

5   The first document is an example of how a 'written requisition' might look. Is it legally correct?

6   The second document is an example of how a 'messenger's authority' might look. Is it legal?

7   Pethidine is a Schedule 2 controlled drug, so an entry of the supply needs to be made in the controlled drug register. Use the example of a page from the controlled drug register in Chapter 16 to make an 'entry.'

8   What should be done with the written requisition and messenger's authority? Do any other entries have to be made?

What further issues should I consider?

■   You now need to look carefully at the documents provided, and decide whether or not the details that they contain fulfil the requirements that you have stated in your answers to the earlier part of the question – in other words, try to apply the knowledge that you have gained to foresee what might happen in the practice of community pharmacy.

1   As the supply is to a practitioner, in this case a doctor, who will use the supply in his or her professional duties, it is an example of a wholesale supply.

2   The supply is exempt from the normal restrictions on the retail supply of medicines because the person purchasing the controlled drug (the doctor) will either administer or supply the drug to a patient. Because he is not using it himself, but in his business (profession), this becomes a wholesale supply.

3   No – she is not a practitioner and she does not have a prescription for the drug.

4

(a)   We have already seen that the pharmacist can act as the supplier of a drug to someone who will use it in their business or profession. Although strictly a wholesale supply, the pharmacist does not need a licence so long as it is only a small part of his or her business. The pharmacist is not a practitioner, so must have received a 'requisition in writing' before he or she (the pharmacist) can deliver the drug to the recipient, in this case the practitioner, Dr Cureall. However, if the recipient can convince you that a genuine emergency exists, and promises to supply the requisition within 24 hours, it is possible to make the wholesale supply without the written requisition, so long as you are convinced that the doctor and the request are genuine. An important point to note is that this facility exists only for wholesale supplies directly to the practitioner for use in their practice – *not* for prescription requests to a patient.

(b)   As we have already seen, Dr Cureall is personally authorised to possess the drugs, so you, as a pharmacist, can supply them to him. Looking back at Question 16, you will find several examples of when a wholesale supply is legally made via a third party – when a pharmacist has ordered controlled drugs from the wholesaler, for example. The van driver whose job it is to deliver the order is acting as a carrier. Anyone who does not normally work as a carrier of wholesale supplies needs written evidence that they are authorised to possess the drug when transporting it. The piece of paper is commonly known as a 'messenger's authority'. In this example, Mrs Deacon is acting as an intermediary in the supply, because it is a wholesale supply and she is transporting controlled drugs, and so she needs written authority to say she is authorised to possess the drug as the 'messenger'.

Do not forget that when someone is transporting a controlled drug to a person with a prescription – and is therefore authorised to have it in their possession – the person transporting the drug does not need any written authorisation to carry it.

5   The requirements for a written requisition are:

- The authority must be signed by the recipient. In the example, the written (not necessarily hand-written, unlike a prescription for pethidine) requisition is signed, and as you know Dr Cureall and his normal signature you will be able to fulfil the requirement to be 'reasonably satisfied that it is genuine'. If the practitioner was not known to you, it would be necessary to take reasonable precautions to check that the practitioner was genuine and that the signature was authentic.
- The authority must state the recipient's name, address and profession – all of which are present in the sample. (It is acceptable to provide details of qualifications to indicate profession.)
- The total quantity of the drug must be specified as the number of ampoules and the amount of drug in each.
- The purpose must be stated – for use in the surgery is adequate.

As all the details necessary are given, the written requisition is legally correct.

6   There are a few legal requirements that must be fulfilled before the 'messenger's authority' is accepted as legal and genuine.

- It must be signed by the recipient – the person who is authorised to possess the controlled drug.
- It must state that the messenger is empowered to receive the drug on behalf of the recipient.

Both of these requirements are fulfilled by the second document, so Mrs Deacon can be given the suitably labelled pethidine ampoules to take back to the surgery. It would be appropriate to ask Mrs Deacon for some identification if you do not know her.

7   Below is an example of a controlled drugs register. Remember that the recipient, Dr Cureall, is the person being supplied, not his receptionist, Mrs Deacon.

RECORD OF* *Pethidine and its salts* SOLD OR SUPPLIED

Date on which transaction was effected	Persons or firm supplied		Particulars as to licence or authority or person or firm to be in possession	Amount supplied	Form in which supplied
	Name	Address			
Today's date	Dr S L Cureall	The Surgery, 17 Main Rd, Anytown	General Practitioner	200 mg	2 Amps Pethidine HCl 100 mg

* *completed by the pharmacist*

8   Both the written requisition and messenger's authority need to be kept for two years. As an entry is made in the controlled drugs register, there is no legal need to make a separate entry of the transaction in the prescription-only register.

Question

19

The sale and supply of spirits in England, Wales and Scotland

You will no doubt be aware that the sale of alcoholic beverages is restricted; for example, no one under the age of 18 is permitted to buy them. There are further controls imposed by the need to account for the duty that is payable to the government. Consequently, any sale of preparations for medicinal use containing a large proportion of alcohol, such as surgical spirits, is also subject to controls. The following questions apply to the legislation in England, Wales and Scotland unless otherwise stated.

Decide whether each of the following statements is true or false. You might also like to make a note of any reasons for, or qualifications of, your chosen answer.

STATEMENT   1   Products containing ethyl alcohol (ethanol) are considered to be intoxicating liquors; their sale is controlled only by the Customs and Excise Management Act 1979.

2   Any pharmacist who wants to sell alcoholic tonic wine has to apply for a licence from the appropriate justice.

3   Pharmacists can dispense a medicine containing a 'spirit' such as brandy.

4   Pharmacists in England and Wales are subject to the same restrictions as other retailers for mineralised methylated spirits, which means that they cannot sell a bottle of 'meths' for a child's steam engine on a Saturday at 10 a.m.

5   Pharmacists in Scotland are subject to the same restrictions as other retailers for mineralised methylated spirits, which means that they cannot sell a bottle of 'meths' to a child of 12 for his steam engine.

6   A pharmacist who wants to stock industrial methylated spirits (IMS) for medicinal purposes has to obtain permission in writing from the national headquarters of HM Customs and Excise.

7   The letter of authority from HM Customs and Excise will specify the exact conditions under which the pharmacist is permitted to keep IMS.

8   A customer can buy IMS.

9   Once the pharmacist is authorised to keep IMS, he or she has to order it from the local authorised methylator.

10   Records must be kept of all supplies to the pharmacy of IMS; these must be kept for two years.

11   If a supply of IMS is made according to a prescription, a record must be made of the amount supplied in the prescription-only register.

12   If a supply of IMS is made to a local practitioner, the amount must not exceed 5 litres.

13   An athlete who wishes to buy some surgical spirit in Glasgow to rub on his feet before a marathon race must sign the prescription-only register; this is not necessary for an athlete wishing to make the same purchase locally before running in the London marathon.

14   The athlete in statement 13 would have to go to a pharmacy in both instances.

What issues should I consider?

■   Think about the controls on the sale and supply of IMS, surgical spirits and 'meths'.

Where should I look in Pharmacy Law & Ethics?

Chapter 24 describes the relevant legislation.

1   False

They are also controlled under the Spirits Regulations 1952, the Alcoholic Liquors Act 1979 and other regulations and notices.

2   True

A pharmacist is not exempt from the normal regulations that apply to other retailers. In England and Wales it is the licensing justices and in Scotland the licensing court that grants the licence.

3   True

Although this type of prescription is much less common than it used to be (owing to the availability of products that control pain more effectively), it can still be prescribed. For examples, look in an old edition of *Martindale: The Extra Pharmacopoeia* for a 'Brompton cocktail' recipe. If such a medicine is dispensed, a pharmacist can claim back the duty paid on the brandy.

4   False

Pharmacists are subject to the same restrictions on the sale of 'meths' as other retailers. It cannot be sold from 10 p.m. on Saturday until Monday at 8 a.m.

5   True

There used to be many more restrictions on the sale of 'meths' in Scotland, which have been relaxed by new legislation in 1998. However, the ban on selling it to anyone under 14 is still in force.

6   False

The pharmacist has to apply to the local Customs and Excise office on the required form, which is available from the same office.

7   True

The conditions will vary from office to office, but will cover storage, use, labelling and supply.

8   False

No, because the amount of duty that is paid is much less than on alcohol for consumption, which is why there is such strict control and why HM Customs and Excise has the right to inspect the records that are kept at any reasonable time.

9   False

A pharmacist who wants to order 20 litres or more must order it from the methylator. However, quantities of less than 20 litres can be ordered from the local wholesaler just like medicines.

10   True

The records must be accessible to the Customs and Excise inspector at all reasonable times.

11   False

However, a record must be made of supplies other than on prescription, for example, to a practitioner.

12   False

The amount must not exceed 3 litres. It is also important to note that the term 'practitioner' has a meaning different from that from the Medicines Act, and includes nurses and chiropodists.

13   True

Again, there used to be additional controls on the sale of 'meths' and surgical spirits in Scotland, which included the recording of such a sale, but the change in the legislation applies to surgical spirits too. No entry is necessary.

14   False

The athlete *could* go to a pharmacist lawfully conducting a retail pharmacy business in Scotland or in England; additional sellers in Scotland no longer have to be registered, as in England.

Question
20

The sale of non-medicinal poisons: general

There are very specific rules that apply to the sales of substances classified as poisons (the Poisons Rules). Before considering the restrictions in detail, decide whether each of the following statements about poisons in general is true or false. You might also like to make a note of any reasons for, or qualifications of, your chosen answer.

STATEMENT

1   The Poisons Act 1972 is also law in Northern Ireland.

2   The Poisons Board is an advisory committee that must include at least five people appointed by the RPSGB.

3   A non-medicinal poison is defined as a substance listed in Part I or Part II of the Poisons List. Other substances, however toxic, are not poisons.

4   Some substances that are poisons are also medicinal products, in which case they are controlled by both acts.

5   All the definitions of 'wholesale dealing' from the Medicines Act also apply to the sale of poisons.

6   Part I poisons are those substances in the Poisons List that can only be sold by pharmacists.

7   Part II poisons are those substances in the Poisons List that can be sold by pharmacists and by 'listed' sellers of poisons, the list being held by the local authority.

8   The inspectors appointed by the RPSGB to enforce the Poisons Act 1972 and rules have no other duties; they may also be appointed by the local authority to also inspect Part II sellers.

9   The Act does not give powers of inspection and/or entry to the premises of a vet, doctor or dentist (unless the premises are a shop).

What issues should I consider?

■   Think about the definition of a 'poison' and who can sell poisons.

Where should I look in Pharmacy Law & Ethics?

The definition of the term 'poison' is explained in Chapter 17, together with details about the different categories of sellers and how the Act is enforced.

Answers and Explanations

20

1   **False**

There is no extension to Northern Ireland, unlike the Medicines Act.

2   **True**

There are at least 16 members in all, although more may be appointed. The RPSGB appoints five of the members.

3   **True**

This is the only definition; to be classified a poison, a substance must be included in the Poisons List.

4   False

In these circumstances, the medicinal product would be controlled by the Medicines Act only; the exact controls would be determined by the use of the substance.

An example would be nicotine, which appears in both the list of medicines for human use and the list of non-medicinal poisons. A form of nicotine is present in the special patches which are applied to the skin by those trying to give up smoking. The nicotine is gradually released into the body of the smoker to help prevent the cravings due to nicotine withdrawal. The nicotine patches are licensed medicinal products.

Nicotine is also present in a variety of dusts that are used in agriculture and horticulture; products with a nicotine content of more than 4% are classified as Schedule 1 poisons. Tobacco products such as cigarettes are classified as Schedule 4 poisons and are therefore exempt from the restrictions.

5   False

Although the Poisons Act uses many of the definitions of the Medicines Act – for example, for 'persons lawfully conducting a retail pharmacy business' – the definition of wholesale dealing is restricted to selling a poison only for the person who buys it to sell it again.

'Administration' in this context means ingestion in some way by a human being, so poisons are not 'administered' (or, if they are, they are restricted under the Medicines Act) and that definition does not apply.

6   True

By pharmacists, we mean, as always, 'persons lawfully conducting a retail pharmacy business'.

7   True

The list is open to inspection and includes details of the premises and of the names of the persons listed.

8   False

The pharmaceutical inspectors also have duties under the Medicines Act and Misuse of Drugs Act, but may, subject to the approval of the RPSGB, undertake to inspect local authority-listed sellers too.

9   **True**

The requirements under the Poisons Act are different to those of the Medicines Act.

The Poisons Rules and Schedules

The Poisons Rules enable a variety of controls to be applied to substances that have already been defined as poisons. In particular, provision is made to apply extra controls to especially dangerous substances by including them in one of the Schedules to the Poisons Rules.

The first part of the question looks at the requirements of the Rules; the second part considers the extra controls imposed by the Schedules.

1   The list below is of items to do with the sale and supply of poisons that the Poisons Rules control; for each of the items on the list, make a relevant comment that is mentioned in the Rules.

(a)   Containers.
(b)   Sales of Part I poisons.
(c)   Sale of Part II poisons.
(d)   Storage.
(e)   Record keeping.

2   The poison, whether in Part I or II, can have Schedule(s) attached to it, which dictate the extra level of control the poison is subject to when it is supplied. Although there were originally 12 Schedules, numbers 2, 3, 6 and 7 no longer apply. For each of the Schedules listed, *either* provide a condition of supply that is applicable and an example of a poison that is subject to that schedule (Schedules 1, 4 and 5) or describe the purpose of the Schedule (Schedules 8–12 inclusive).

At this stage, try to think of a brief comment to make about the schedule; more comprehensive details of certain Schedule 1 poisons will be considered in Question 22 and at Level 2.

(a)   Schedule 1.
(b)   Schedule 4, group 1.
(c)   Schedule 4, group 2.
(d)   Schedule 5.
(e)   Schedule 8.

(f)   Schedule 9.
(g) Schedule 10.
(h) Schedule 11.
(i)   Schedule 12.

What issues should I consider?

■   In addition to an understanding of the term poison and the general restrictions on the sale of poisons, you need to be able to apply the Rules and Schedules to be able to conform to all the legally necessary restrictions on the sale and supply of very dangerous substances.

Where should I look in Pharmacy Law & Ethics?

The Poisons Rules and the Schedules are described in Chapter 17. You will also need to refer to Appendices 12 and 13.

Answers and Explanations

21

1

(a) The Poisons Rules used to require that small quantities of poisons were supplied in vertically ribbed containers so as to be distinguishable by touch; the control now lies with the Chemicals Regulations, which require a tactile warning on the packaging of specified substances.

(b) A Part I poison must be sold by a pharmacist from his or her registered premises.

(c) A Part II poison must be sold by the listed seller or one of the two 'responsible deputies' he or she appoints to sell poisons in his or her absence, or by a pharmacist.

(d) Schedule 1 poisons must be stored separately from foods and other items.

(e) The Rules describe for how long the various records that need to kept should be stored – this is generally two years.

2

(a) Schedule 1. The conditions that apply concern the keeping of records, storage and very specific conditions of sale, which are covered in detail in Question 22. Lots of examples could be chosen from the list in Appendix 13.

(b) Schedule 4, group 1. This Schedule covers substances that are exempt from control even though they contain poisons, because of the way in which they are used, for example, fire extinguishers containing barium chloride.

(c)   Schedule 4, group 2. This Schedule covers substances that are exempt because they contain only a very small amount of substance or a particular formulation of it, for example, seed treatments containing drazoxolon.

(d)   Schedule 5. This Schedule covers those poisons that listed sellers are only allowed to sell in certain forms or to certain people. Other than in these circumstances, these poisons must be sold from pharmacies. An example of such a poison is oxamyl, in preparations for use only in agriculture and horticulture.

(e)   Schedule 8. This Schedule is the form to be used in an application to a local authority to become a listed seller of Part II poisons. An example is given in Appendix 13.

(f)   Schedule 9. This Schedule specifies the way in which the list of listed sellers of Part II poisons must be kept by the local authority. An example is given in Appendix 13.

(g)   Schedule 10. This Schedule is the certificate necessary for the purchase of a Schedule 1 poison when the purchaser is not known to the pharmacist. An example is given in Appendix 13.

(h)   Schedule 11. This Schedule specifies the way in which a record of the sale of a Schedule 1 poison must be made in the poisons register. An example is given in Appendix 13.

(i)   Schedule 12. This Schedule is the form used for the purchase of Schedule 1 poisons to which extra controls apply. The form has various parts; the one that is completed depends on which compound is being sold. An example of the entire form is given in Appendix 13.

Question 22

The sale of Schedule 1 poisons

Before a Schedule 1 poison can be sold, the pharmacist must be sure that the person to whom the sale is made is someone who can be trusted to handle the poison responsibly. If the person is not known to the pharmacist, another person who is known to the pharmacist has to vouch for the purchaser. This question looks at a 'flow chart' of the procedures that need to be followed in each eventuality.

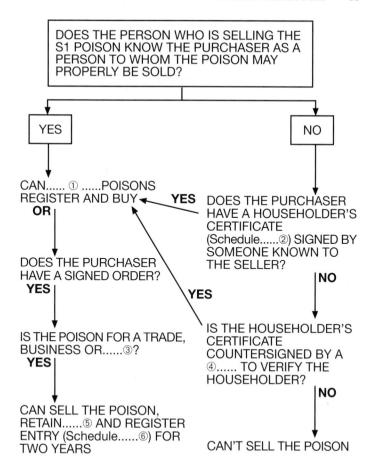

Study it carefully and then insert the appropriate words represented by the numbers 1 to 6.

What issues should I consider?

- Apart from the difficulties of complying with the law on selling Schedule 1 poisons, there are also problems caused by the language that is used. To be able to understand terms such as a 'householder' you may need to consult a dictionary; in order to realise the historical significance of a householder as being a person who can vouch for another, an encyclopaedia may be more appropriate.

Where should I look in Pharmacy Law & Ethics?

Chapter 17 describes the regulations governing the sale of Schedule 1 poisons and the necessary paperwork.

Answers   1   Sign.
and   2   Schedule 10.
Explanations 3   Profession.
22   4   Police officer.
                 5   Signed order.
                 6   Schedule 11.

Question

23

The sale of Schedule 1 poisons with extra controls

Some substances are so poisonous that even the controls on Schedule 1 poisons (Question 22) are insufficient; the questions below relate to the extra legal restrictions on some of the substances, which are described fully in Chapter 17.

1   Name the Schedule 1 substances that are controlled by Schedule 12.
2   Very briefly describe two of the circumstances in which the extra controls on the sale of these substances do not apply.
3   Name the conditions associated with each of the following aspects of the sale of strychnine as a pesticide for killing moles.

(a)   The legally necessary authorisations.
(b)   The container.
(c)   The labelling.

What issues should I consider?

■   Think about the legal restrictions on the sale of Schedule 1 poisons that have already been covered.
■   Reflect on the compounds that are classified as Schedule 1 with extra controls, and the very complicated paperwork described in Schedule 12 (which is different for each substance), which must be completed exactly correctly before any of them can be supplied. Then consider the further conditions that are imposed by other legislation on these substances, even when they are sold for the use specified.

Where should I look in Pharmacy Law & Ethics?

The sale of Schedule 1 poisons with extra controls is covered in Chapter 17.

**Answers
and
Explanations**

23

1   Strychnine, fluoroacetic acid, zinc phosphide, calcium, potassium and sodium cyanides, sodium and potassium arsenites and thallium. The cyanides are sold only under a special exemption, which is covered in Question 13 at Level 2.

2   Exemptions to the extra controls of Schedule 12 apply in the following situations:

•   when sold for export;
•   when sold for the purposes of research or chemical analysis.

3

(a)   Two *additional* forms (remember that for a Schedule 1 poison a Schedule 10 is needed if the purchaser is not known to the pharmacist, and a 'signed order' may be supplied) are needed:

(i)   to satisfy the Poisons Rules, Schedule 12, Part II, must be duly signed and presented within three months of the date on it;

(ii) to satisfy the pesticides legislation, the purchaser must have a written authority issued by, for England, a person authorised by the Ministry of Agriculture, Fisheries and Food (now the Department for Environment, Food and Rural Affairs) or, for Scotland, the Department of Agriculture and Fisheries and, for Wales, the Welsh Office Agricultural Department.

(b)   It must be packed in quantities not exceeding 2 g; quantities of more than 8 g can only be sold to providers of a commercial service.

(c)   The strychnine must be in the original packaging as supplied by the manufacturer, with an approved label.

Question

24

The sale of chemicals

Pharmacists are sometimes asked to sell chemicals which, although they are not classified as poisons under the Poisons Act 1972, can be dangerous under certain circumstances; great care must be taken to ensure that any member of the public wishing to purchase chemicals is aware of the potential dangers and is not going to use them for an unsuitable purpose. Chemicals and solvents are not to be sold to anyone under 16.

Decide whether each of the following statements is true or false. You might also like to make a note of any reasons for, or qualifications of, your chosen answer.

STATEMENT

1   The primary purpose of the Chemicals Hazard Information and Packaging Regulations 1994 (CHIP regulations) is to determine whether or not a substance is dangerous to health if it is inhaled.

2   There are two main categories of danger – danger due to the chemical nature of the substance and danger to health.

3   If you order a chemical to supply to a member of the public, the manufacturer is responsible for classification and labelling, so the pharmacist does not need to check any further.

4   A data sheet must be supplied to members of the public who purchase a chemical for use in the home.

5   Business purchasers of chemicals must be supplied with any updated data sheets regarding the chemical they have purchased.

What issues should I consider?

■   Think about the level of danger the chemical could pose to people or the environment.

■   What information about the chemical must be given to its potential user?

Where should I look in Pharmacy Law & Ethics?

Chapter 18 describes the supply of chemicals controlled by CHIP and CoSHH regulations. For a detailed list of such substances, refer to Appendix 14.

Answers and Explanations

24

1   **False**

There are two main objectives of CHIP regulations, namely to prevent danger to people and the environment and to remove barriers to trade in the EU. This is achieved by regulations concerning the classification of a substance that has been assessed as dangerous into one of two main categories of danger and ensuring that the substance is packaged, labelled and transported safely.

2   **True**

Each of the main categories of danger is then subdivided according to its effect on health, whether it is an oxidising agent, etc.

3   False

Responsibility is transferred down the chain of supply, so a pharmacist must obtain chemicals from a reputable supplier or check independently as the final supplier and take responsibility for any errors.

4   False

Labelling is considered to be 'sufficient information' provided a reference to any particular conditions of use is given on the label. A 'safety data sheet' could be supplied, even though this is not legally necessary except when used in business.

5   True

In order to comply with the requirement to issue revised data sheets to any business customers who have been supplied within the last 12 months, pharmacists are advised to keep records of such sales.

2

Level Two

You will no doubt have read the introduction to the whole text which explains that the exercises at Level 2 are intended to assist preregistration trainees to understand pharmacy law and ethics. There are some extra points to note about the intentions of the exercises in Level 2. In order to meet the demands of the RPSGB programme for both the work-based components and the registration exam, you will need to understand how to apply much of the theoretical knowledge in practice situations; consequently, a 'problem solving' approach is the most appropriate. The intention of the registration exam is to test the 'higher level' skills of analysis and evaluation, which is supported by the use of multiple choice questions (MCQs). The exercises that follow include examples of different types of questions; some are presented in the format used by the registration exam, which is explained below. For further details of the requirements of the syllabus and of the exam, refer to the preregistration trainees portfolio and workbook, and the *Pharmacy Preregistration Handbook*, second edition.

Instructions to enable you to answer the four different types of MCQs used in the registration exam

In both the open-book and the closed-book registration examination papers, there are four different types of MCQs. The instructions for each type are given on the paper before a set of similar questions, and a summary is given on each page. If you look at the sample papers sent to all preregistration trainees by the RPSGB you will find examples of each type of question, together with the relevant instructions.

We have set some of the Level 2 questions as MCQs, to give you practice at answering them. The instructions for each type are given below and referred to in each exercise as appropriate.

Type 1 – simple completion

For these questions, you have to read the question carefully and then select the one correct answer from the list given; each possible answer will be labelled A, B, C, D or E.

Type 2 – classification

These are a little different as they have five possible answers (A, B, C, D and E as before) printed before the questions. There will not necessarily be five questions, and you can use the answer codes once, more than once, or not at all.

Type 3 – multiple completion

You will find that these demand even more work, as each question now has three statements, labelled 1, 2 and 3, to accompany it. You have to decide which – and it can be more than one – of the three statements is correct, and then assign your answers a code as follows:

> If statements 1, 2 and 3 are correct, the code is A.
> If statements 1 and 2 are correct, the code is B.
> If statements 2 and 3 are correct, the code is C.
> If statement 1 only is correct, the code is D.
> If statement 3 only is correct, the code is E.

Type 4 – assertion: reason

Most people agree that these are the hardest type of all; again a code needs to be assigned to the right combination of answers.

For each question you will be given two statements; you then have to decide whether each statement is true or false.

You then choose a code as follows:

> If both statements are true and 2 is an explanation of 1, then the code is A.
> If both statements are true and 2 is not an explanation of 1, then the code is B.
> If statement 1 is true and statement 2 is false, then the code is C.
> If statement 1 is false and statement 2 is true, then the code is D.
> If statement 1 is false and statement 2 is false, then the code is E.

Question 1

Applying the definitions of the Medicines Act 1968 to help in an everyday situation

In order to deal with the following request you will need to revise the definitions used in the Medicines Act.

1   A dentist requests you, the preregistration trainee, to make up 500 ml of normal saline (it contains 0.9% w/v Sodium Chloride BP in purified water), for use in his/her practice. The only pharmacist is out at lunch. Explain fully, with reasons, whether or not you would supply it in the pharmacist's absence.

2   If a doctor wishes to buy normal saline injections for use in a nebuliser, would the situation be any different? Briefly explain your answer.

What issues should I consider?

- The Medicines Act has a language all of its own. You need to understand how the definitions can be used to help you in everyday situations.
- Once you have reminded yourself of the definitions, decide whether or not the sodium chloride solution would be controlled under the Medicines Act and, if it is, how that would affect your ability to supply it without the pharmacist present.

Where should I look in Pharmacy Law & Ethics?

The index can be used to find the references to the definitions you will need; an explanation is given when each is used for the first time.

Answers and Explanations 1

See Chapter 5 and Question 6 at Level 1 to remind yourself of the way in which the legal classifications of POM, GSL and, by default, P medicinal products arise. You should also remind yourself that every medicinal product made up in a pharmacy, although exempt from the requirements of the Medicines Act to have a marketing authorisation, automatically becomes a pharmacy medicine, so you cannot supply it without the pharmacist being present.

However, if you can definitely say that it is not a medicinal product, and is therefore exempt from the legal classifications of the Medicines Act, you could supply it – in the same way that foods, vitamins and cosmetics are exempt under certain circumstances and can be sold from premises other than pharmacies.

The next step is to re-examine the definitions of a 'medicinal product'.

The sodium chloride solution is a medicinal product if it is to be given to human(s) for a medicinal purpose or if it to be used as an ingredient administered by a practitioner.

You now need to answer the questions.

1   As the solution is for a dentist, it is likely to be used for humans, so may well be treating or preventing disease – a medicinal purpose. In this case, it must be a P medicinal product and the pharmacist must supervise the sale. However, it could be wanted for a use other than for a medicinal purpose, for example, for rinsing out equipment. In this case, though, it would be very hard to prove that it is not intended for a medicinal purpose if it is bought for use in practice. The best policy is always to err on the side of caution, so say you will make it up, get it checked by the pharmacist and take it round as soon as possible.

2   The sale of sodium chloride solution in injectable form is a much easier situation – it is listed in the *Medicines, Ethics & Practice* guide as a POM (as are all injectable substances for human use) and can only be sold to the doctor by the pharmacist in person. The fact that the injections are being sold to a practitioner for another use makes no difference.

Question
2

A summary of the conditions affecting the sale of P and GSL medicinal products

Test your knowledge of the legal requirements for selling medicines by answering the following; you might find it useful to try this as a revision exercise without using any reference sources.

1   Give the exact legal classification(s) for each of the following preparations:

(a)   32 non-effervescent paracetamol and codeine (co-codamol 8/500) tablets.

(b)   24 effervescent aspirin tablets 300 mg.

(c)   Ibuprofen gel.

2   Give two conditions for each of the preparations in (1) above that must be met before a sale to the public can legally be made. Do not include any labelling requirements in your answers; each of the six conditions must be different.

*What
issues
should I
consider?*
Consider all the factors that affect the sale of General Sale List (GSL) and Pharmacy (P) medicines, such as:

- The type of premises.
- The presence of a pharmacist.
- The terms of the marketing authorisation.
- The definitions of maximum daily dose (mdd), maximum dose (md) and maximum strength (ms).
- The use of the product.
- The size of the pack, especially with preparations of paracetamol and aspirin.

*Where should
I look in
Pharmacy
Law & Ethics?*
You will need to use the index for the definitions of md, mdd and ms. Chapter 5 deals with the sale of P medicines and Chapter 6 with those classified as GSL. For details of the legal restrictions on each of the products you will have to refer to *Medicines, Ethics & Practice*; it may also be necessary to refer to the Summary of Product Characteristics.

**Answers
and
Explanations**

2

The table below represents the conditions for sale that may be used. For some, conditions 1 and 2 are interchangeable; other answers are specific to that preparation.

	Exact legal classification	*Condition 1 that must be met in order that a sale can legally take place*	*Condition 2 that must be met before a sale can legally take place*
24 co-codamol tablets	CD Inv P	Keep invoice for two years	Pharmacist in a position to intervene/supervise before sale can be made
24 effervescent aspirin tablets, 300 mg	GSL	Must be sold from a lockable shop or a machine that is situated in a position from where the public can be excluded	Must have a marketing authorisation
Ibuprofen gel	If P	The ms must not exceed 10% w/w of ibuprofen	It must be sold for external use only
	If GSL	Any two from: ms 5%/ for a person over 12/ mdd 500 mg/md 125 mg/not more than 2.5 g in pack	

Question

3

Under what circumstances can a controlled drug be sold as a P medicine?

The concept of certain controlled drugs being available as POMs or P medicines has already been covered at Level 1, in Question 9. You will need to use that knowledge in order to be able to answer this MCQ type 3. Refer to the instructions on answering the different types of MCQ on p.64. You will also need to use a BNF to find out the strength of standard preparations.

Which of the following statements in Question 3 is/are true?

Question

3.1

STATEMENT   1   Pholcodine Linctus BP is classified as a CD Inv P because the concentration of pholcodine is less than 1.5% w/v.

2   If a new pholcodine linctus were formulated to contain 15 mg/5 ml, it would contain 3% w/v pholcodine.

3   A new pholcodine linctus containing 15 mg/5 ml would be a CD Inv POM if the dose was 10 ml three times a day.

Question

3.2

STATEMENT   1   Pholcodine Linctus, Strong, BP, is a CD Inv P at the dose recommended in the BNF.

2   If Pholcodine Linctus, Strong, BP, is given with a recommended dose of 10 ml, it is classified as a CD Inv POM.

3   Kaolin and morphine mixture must contain less than 0.04% w/v anhydrous morphine in order for it to be classified as a CD Inv P.

Question

3.3

STATEMENT   1   Dihydrocodeine is one of a list of six controlled drugs that can, under certain circumstances, be classified as a CD Inv POM or a CD Inv P.

2   Dihydrocodeine is available in an over-the-counter (OTC) preparation called Paramol.

3   A tablet must weigh at least 600 mg if the md and ms of dihydrocodeine it can contain to be legally available over the counter are not to be exceeded.

Question

3.4

STATEMENT

1   Oramorph oral solution is a CD Inv POM because the concentration of morphine is below 0.2% w/v anhydrous morphine but above 0.02%, and also because the morphine cannot be readily recovered in an amount likely to constitute a danger to health.

2   Oramorph concentrated oral solution is a CD POM drug because the concentration of anhydrous morphine is greater than 0.2% w/v.

3   The Oramorph oral solution could be supplied to a member of the public as an 'emergency supply at the request of a patient', so long as the conditions of such supplies were met, but the concentrated solution cannot be supplied to a member of the public by a pharmacist under any circumstances without a valid prescription.

What issues should I consider?

■   An understanding of what is meant by basic terms such as concentration and strength, expressed as both percentages and dose per unit volume, together with the Medicines Act definitions of md, mdd and ms, is vital.

■   You will also need to know the difference between a base and an anhydrous salt.

■   Consider the specific conditions that apply to each of the controlled drugs in question.

■   You will also need to know the conditions under which emergency supplies of POMs can be made.

Where should I look in Pharmacy Law & Ethics?

Most of the necessary information to enable you work out the answers is given in Chapter 7.

To find out the concentration of pholcodine in a preparation such as pholcodine linctus, you will need to use a BNF.

**Answers
and
Explanations**

3

**Answers
and
Explanations**

3.1

1   False

From the BNF, Pholcodine Linctus BP contains 5 mg/5 ml, so the concentration is only 0.1% w/v, but there is also another condition – the md must be 20 mg.

2   False

15 mg in 5 ml is 0.3% w/v (1 g in 100 ml is 1%).

3   True

Pholcodine is a CD POM, but if for non-parenteral use and in undivided preparations of ms 2.5%, it is a CD Inv POM, with no md.
       Code = E (3 only is correct).

**Answers
and
Explanations**

3.2

1   True

The strength is 10 mg/5 ml, which is 0.2% w/v, i.e. <1.5%. In addition, the recommended dose is 5 ml three to four times daily, which gives a dose of 10 mg – less than the md of 20 mg, so it fulfils both the requirements for being a CD Inv P.

2   False

The preparation contains 10 mg/5 ml of pholcodine, so 10 ml gives exactly 20 mg, so the md is not exceeded. Another point to note is that as no salt is mentioned, it can be assumed that the preparation contains 10 mg/5 ml of the anhydrous base, which is what the classification depends on.

3   False

The concentration of morphine that determines whether or not the preparation is CD Inv POM or CD Inv P, i.e. the ms, is 0.02%. In a solid preparation the ms is 0.04%.
       Code = D (1 only is correct).

Answers and Explanations

3.3

1   True

2   True

Preparations and their contents are listed in the BNF.

3   False

The md of dihydrocodeine to be a CD Inv P is 10 mg and the ms is 1.5%. If 10 mg represents 1.5% of the tablet's weight, then 100% is 10 x100/1.5 = 666.67 mg. In other words, if the md of 10 mg is present, and the ms is 1.5%, the tablet must weigh at least 666.67 mg or the sale of the tablet as a CD Inv P will be illegal; the commercially available preparation contains 500 mg of paracetamol and only 7.46 mg of dihydrocodeine.
    Code = B (1 and 2 are correct).

Answers and Explanations

3.4

1   True

The ms for a preparation to be a CD Inv POM is 0.2% anhydrous morphine; the Oramorph solution contains 10 mg/5 ml morphine sulphate, and so will contain less than 0.2% but more than 0.02% of the base.

2   True

The concentration of anhydrous morphine in Oramorph concentrated solution is 100 mg/5 ml, which is 2%, higher than the ms of 0.2%, so it is a CD POM.

3   True

CD Inv POMs are not controlled drugs. The only requirement that is different to other POMs is to keep the invoice for two years. Emergency supplies can be made, provided all the criteria are met (Question 13, Level 1). No emergency supplies are allowed for CD POMs, and they cannot be supplied unless the prescription is valid.
    Code = A (1, 2 and 3 are correct).

Question

4

A revision exercise in the labelling of P medicines for sale

In Question 7 at Level 1, we considered the labelling requirements for P medicines. Suppose you are in an emergency situation where small packages are being assembled from a large POM pack and labelled ready for sale to the public. (If it were a common occurrence, you would need to apply for the appropriate licence.)

For the following questions, decide whether the statements about the 'label' below are true or false; you may qualify your answer, but remember that in the registration examination you will need to decide one way or the other, even if you consider the question to be ambiguous.

---

50 Asprin tablets effervescent 300 mg BP

Dose: For the secondary prevention of myocardial infarction, 150 mg to be
taken every day, preferably after breakfast.

Not to be taken by children under 12, or those who have or are suffering from stomach ulcers. May not be appropriate for those with asthma.

To be taken with or after food. Dissolve or mix with water before taking.

|CONTAINS ASPIRIN|

EXPIRY DATE JUNE 2005   MA 0000/1234   BN 0001

Made by: Any Pharmaceuticals plc, Anytown, England, on behalf of the Marketing Authorisation Holders, Everytown Pharmacies plc

---

STATEMENT

1   The common name of the medicinal product does not need to be included, as the name of the product is not an invented name.

2   A statement as to the active ingredients is given qualitatively and quantitatively.

3   There is no excipient stated; all those with a recognised action must be stated.

4   The directions concerning the route, method of administration and self-administration instructions are sufficient.

5   All the special warnings that might need to be included are present.

6   The expiry date is on the label.

7   The warning label(s) are those required by the additional special requirements for certain GSL medicines.

8   The words 'contains aspirin' are not needed.

*What
issues
should I
consider?*

You will need to consider all the factors described in Question 7 at Level 1; you might like to revise them and then try to answer the questions without referring to *Pharmacy Law and Ethics*, as in the 'closed-book' examination.

*Where should
I look in
Pharmacy
Law & Ethics?*

Chapter 14 describes the labelling of relevant medicinal products.

**Answers
and
Explanations**

4

The numbers in brackets refer to the standard labelling particulars.

Refer also to Question 7 at Level 1 for full explanations of the points raised.

1　False

If the name of the product on the label was spelt correctly, i.e. 'aspirin', this statement would be true. Check carefully again!

2　False

The abbreviation of the strength (i.e. asp(i)rin tablets 300 mg BP) on the label is used on dispensed medicines, but it is not correct for medicines that are sold. The quantity per dosage unit – i.e. in each tablet – must be clearly stated (2), and a reference to the quality of the active ingredient given; in this case it would be Aspirin BP.

3　True

The necessity to include excipients is described in point (4).

4　True

However, whether or not they are 'comprehensible' – a general labelling requirement – is open to question. These tablets would normally only be sold to those who specifically request them on medical advice, as they are cheaper to buy than the current prescription charge. They can also be taken for their anticoagulant properties in other conditions, so it may be appropriate to put that on the label too.

5　False

The special warnings that could be a condition of the marketing authorisation are indeed present (7), but all medicinal products are required to have a special warning that the product should be stored out of the reach of children, and this is not present (6).

6   True

But it is required to be stated in clear terms and, because of the size of the print in this case, probably does not fulfil the requirement (8).

7   False

The label bears the cautionary labels which must be affixed to the product when it is dispensed. The warning label for aspirin required by the additional regulations for GSL medicines, in this case, is 'If symptoms persist, consult your doctor', together with the recommended dosage (1). The warning should be in a rectangular box in which there is no other matter, and in a prominent position. As the product is GSL but the pack size means it can only be sold from pharmacies, the label must have a 'P' in a rectangle too.

8   True

The name of the product contains the word aspirin (assuming it had been spelt correctly), so making it clear what the tablets contain – by including this warning – is not legally necessary.

Question

5

A summary of labelling requirements

The following type 3 MCQs test your knowledge of all the labelling regulations for a variety of relevant medicinal products; refer to the general instructions on MCQs for the correct codes to use.

Question

5.1

With regard to the standard labelling requirements for relevant medicinal products for human use:

STATEMENT

1   A pictogram can be included on a label in order to clarify the information given.

2   If a medicinal product is available in more than one strength, an indication of the strength must be included in the name of the medicinal product.

3   The outer packaging may include information that is useful for health education, provided that it is for clarification and not promotional reasons.

Question

5.2

With regard to the standard labelling requirements for relevant medicinal products for human use:

STATEMENT

1 All eye drops must be labelled to show the excipients which are active ingredients.
2 The labels of every medicinal product must state all the active ingredients, including all the excipients.
3 Any person who contravenes the labelling regulations can be fined £5000 and be sentenced to two years' imprisonment.

Question

5.3

With regard to the standard labelling requirements for relevant medicinal products for human use:

STATEMENT

1 The 'common name' is defined under the Medicines Act as the proprietary name.
2 When a medicinal product is assembled for sale in a pharmacy, the name and address of the shop that supplies the medication must be on the label.
3 The labelling regulations for a medicinal product that is sold must have the quantity of the product by weight, by volume or by the number of doses of the product; this is not the case for dispensed medicinal products.

Question

5.4

With regard to the standard labelling requirements for relevant medicinal products for human use:

STATEMENT

1 The holder of a marketing authorisation who proposes to alter the labelling of a medicinal product may do so provided that:

> The marketing authorisation holder has not been notified to the contrary within a period of 90 days from the time of notification of the licensing authority.

2 The only general labelling provisions are that the label is easily legible, comprehensible and indelible.
3 Vitamin preparations that are exempt from the need for a marketing authorisation are also totally exempt from the labelling requirements for medicinal products.

Question 5.5

With regard to the standard labelling requirements for relevant medicinal products for human use, where a medicinal product is packaged in a blister pack, the minimum requirements are:

STATEMENT

1   The name of the product.
2   The name of the holder of the marketing authorisation.
3   The batch number and expiry date.

Question 5.6

All labels for relevant medicinal products for veterinary use have the following additional requirements:

STATEMENT

1   The words 'For animal treatment only' must be on the label.
2   The address of the owner of the animal must be on the label.
3   The words 'This treatment is for an animal under my care' must be on the label if the medicinal product is a POM.

Question 5.7

When labelling ampoules that are relevant medicinal products for human use, the requirements include:

STATEMENT

1   The name of the medicinal product and the strength.
2   The method of administration.
3   The expiry date and batch number.

Question 5.8

When labelling a 'chemist's nostrum' (a preparation made up by a pharmacist for sale from the pharmacy without a marketing authorisation), the following must be included:

STATEMENT

1   Directions for use.
2   Any special handling and storage requirements.
3   A complete list of all ingredients, including excipients.

What issues should I consider?

■   Take into account all the requirements for the labelling of relevant medicinal products, both for humans and for veterinary use.

Where should I look in Pharmacy Law & Ethics?

Chapter 14 covers all the aspects of labelling necessary.

**Answers
and
Explanations**

A number in brackets refers to the detailed entry in the appropriate section of Chapter 14 regarding labelling.

**Answers
and
Explanations**

5.1

1   True

An example would be the symbol ✋

2   True

This is a new requirement for relevant medicinal products; an example would be the revised labelling of the liquid paracetamol preparations with the proprietary name Calpol. The preparation containing 120 mg/5 ml is known as Calpol Paediatric suspension and the 250 mg/5 ml version as Calpol Six Plus suspension.

3   True

Generally, there is far more information about the medicinal product available, some of which is accessible to the public who buy it.
Code = A.

**Answers
and
Explanations**

5.2

1   False

Eye drops must be labelled with all the excipients stated (4).

2   False

For preparations other than topical eye preparations and injectables, only the excipients which have a recognised action need to be stated (4).

3   True

Code = E.

**Answers
and
Explanations**

5.3

1   False

The definition states that the common name is the international non-proprietary name (1).

2   False

The name and address must be that of the marketing authorisation holder; the shop name and address may be added as well (11).

3   True

See point (2) for sales. Although it is not a legal requirement for the quantity to be included on dispensed medicines, it is strongly recommended by the RPSGB.
Code = E.

Answers and Explanations 5.4

1   True

2   False

There is also a general requirement that the label is in English and in one or more other languages.

3   False

Even when exempt from the Medicines Act by virtue of their lack of a claim as to a medicinal purpose, vitamins must still follow the guidelines for the labelling of foods and cosmetics.
Code = D.

Answers and Explanations 5.5

1   True

2   True

3   True

These requirements are the minimum that the manufacturer can use.
Code = A.

Answers and Explanations 5.6

1   True

It is also a requirement that these words appear in every leaflet supplied with veterinary medicines.

2   False

The requirement for the animal owner's address to be on the label is for dispensed veterinary medicines only.

3   False

These words need to be on a veterinary prescription for a POM.
Code = E.

Answers and Explanations 5.7

1   False

The strength is only needed when necessary – for example, when there is more than one.

2   True

3   True

It should be noted that there is an additional requirement to those above, namely that the contents of the ampoule are to be stated by weight, volume or unit (5).

     Code = C.

Answers and Explanations

The numbers in brackets refer to section (c) 'other exempt medicinal products'.

1   True

(5).

1   True

(7).

3   False

Only the name of the product (1) and the appropriate quantitative particulars (3) need to be included.

   In addition to these requirements, there are others.

     Code = B.

Question

6

POM medicines: what can legally be supplied to whom?

Use the concepts that were covered in Question 12 at Level 1 to decide which of the following transactions fulfil the legal requirements of the Medicines Act, and then decide whether or not they conform to the Medicines Act definition of a wholesale or retail supply.

   Use the following codes to determine the type of supply (A or E) and legality (B, C or D) of the transactions outlined in the statements below.

     A = Wholesale.
     B = Legal.
     C = Legal but unethical according to RPSGB Code of Ethics.
     D = Illegal.
     E = Retail not wholesale.

Note that, unlike the preregistration examination, these questions will have more than one answer. Classify each one as to what the sale would be if it were made, even if it would be illegal.

1   A doctor who purchases a bottle of amoxycillin syrup to treat her son.
2   A doctor who purchases a pack of Distaclor MR to supply to a patient for his own use.
3   A vet who buys water for injections to give to his wife for use in her nebuliser.
4   A pharmacist who supplies a local 'drug store' with a tube of Betnovate cream to sell.
5   A pharmacist who supplies the local optician with a bottle of chloramphenicol eye drops for his own use.
6   A midwife who wishes to purchase nitrazepam tablets for use in her practice.
7   A chiropodist with a certificate of competence who wishes to purchase lignocaine with adrenaline injections to use on her patients.
8   The carer at a local nursing home who wishes to purchase some Co-Proxamol tablets for a resident in advance of the next prescription.
9   The master of a ship which does not have a doctor on board who wishes to purchase some flucloxacillin capsules for use on a sailor with an infected toe.
10   The professor of pharmacology at your local university who wishes to purchase some prednisolone tablets for use in her research.

What issues should I consider?

■   Think about the reasons for exemption from the restrictions on retail sale and supply under the Medicines Act, and the classes of persons who are exempt.
■   Remember the definition of a wholesale supply under the Medicines Act.

Where should I look in Pharmacy Law & Ethics?

The exemptions from the restrictions on retail sale are covered in Chapter 8.

Answers and Explanations

6

1   A, B

A doctor can purchase any medicinal product; if administered to someone else, it is a wholesale supply.

2   A, B

The explanation is as in 1.

3   A, D

Vets cannot purchase any medicine for use on humans, only for use on animals.

4   A, D

The supply is, of course, illegal; if a supply of a GSL medicinal product was made, it would be a wholesale supply.

5   E, D

Opticians are only allowed to purchase chloramphenicol eye drops for use in their practice, and in an emergency. If the circumstances allowed him to purchase the drops, it would be a retail sale as they would be for the optician's own use.

6   A, D

A midwife may have certain wholesale supplies that are exempt from the normal restrictions, for use in her practice. Nitrazepam tablets are not included in the exemptions.

7   A, B

Chiropodists with a certificate of competence can purchase certain injections for use in their practice, including lignocaine with adrenaline, so long as the strength of adrenaline does not exceed 1 mg per 200 ml.

8   E, D

If this were allowed, it would be a retail sale. If the resident could be interviewed directly, it might be possible to provide an 'emergency supply' but not to sell them.

9   A, B

This is a wholesale supply as the master of the ship will be supplying to someone else, which he is allowed to do if there is no doctor on board.

10   E, B

Universities may purchase POMs for use in research etc., but this does not constitute a wholesale purchase as it is the university that will be using it.

Question

7

The legal requirements for POM prescriptions

In Question 11 at Level 1 the legality of a POM prescription was examined using the requirements for an NHS prescription as an example. For this question, use the following 'private' prescription from the local health centre to test your knowledge.

```
                                                          A M Akroyd

                                                 Mersey Health Centre
                                                        Liverpool St
                                                         ANYTOWN

                                                         Today's date

          Mrs M Morris
          7 Valley Rd
          Anytown

          Supply      42 Prednisolone EC tablets

                             6 daily as directed

                          Repeat as required
                       Signed by A M Akroyd
```

1   What legal omission has been made?
2   What else do you need to know, that is not a legal requirement, before you can dispense the prescription?
3   Although it is not strictly a legal requirement, in Appendix 9 of the BNF there is a list of the cautionary labels pharmacists are recommended to add to dispensed medicinal products. What cautionary labels would you put on this preparation?
4   What records do you need to keep?
5   What do you do with this prescription after you have dispensed it?
6   How many times can it be repeated?
7   How would the procedures outlined in 4, 5 and 6 be different for an NHS prescription?
8   Assuming that the prescription had been written by a vet, what else would legally need to be:
(a)   on the prescription?
(b)   on the label?

What issues should I consider?

■   Review the legal requirements for a prescription for a POM, as determined by the Medicines Act.

Where should I look in Pharmacy Law & Ethics?

This would be a good 'closed-book' revision question.

1   An indication as to the type of practitioner who is writing the prescription.

2   The strength of tablets – 2.5 or 5 mg. It is not a legal requirement for this to be on the prescription, but you need to know the doctor's intentions before it can be dispensed. If the prescriber is not known to you, checks must be made to ensure that the doctor is a registered medical practitioner with an address in the UK.

3   The appropriate cautionary labels for individual preparations are to be found in the BNF, Appendix 9, and the code number is also given with the entry in the appropriate therapeutic section. Most label printing programmes add them automatically. For prednisolone e/c they are:

> Number 5 – do not take indigestion remedies at the same time of day as this medicine.
>
> Number 10 – follow the printed instructions you have been given with this medicine – which refers to the steroid card for long-term use.
>
> Number 25 – to be swallowed whole, not chewed.

4   As this is a private prescription, a record must be made in the prescription-only register and kept for two years.

5   The prescriber has indicated that it is a 'repeatable' prescription, so it may be handed back to the customer so that he or she can obtain the next supply. The patient or customer does not have to return to the same pharmacy.

6   Only once, as there is no direction as to the number of times it can be repeated. The words 'as required' make no difference – the patient can only have it dispensed twice in all.

7   No records are required to be made for NHS prescriptions, which are sent to the Prescription Pricing Authority at the end of the month. NHS prescriptions cannot be repeated.

8

(a)   A veterinary prescription for a POM must contain a declaration that the medicine is for an animal or herd under the vet's care, and the address must be that of the person to whom the medicine is to be delivered.

(b)   A label for a veterinary prescription must include the name and address of the person having charge of the animal or herd, and the words 'For animal treatment only' (unless the label is too small for this to be practicable).

Question 8

The legality of a veterinary prescription for a POM

Although some pharmacists specialise in the fields of agricultural and veterinary medicine, for most, a veterinary prescription is unusual and needs to be checked carefully to ensure that it meets the additional POM requirements. Examine the prescription presented below and then answer the type 4 MCQs that follow.

The Fairway Veterinary Group
Anytown

For Animal Treatment Only

This Treatment Is For An Animal Under My Care

For 'Blackie'
c/o Mrs D Norton
The Common
Anytown

Please Supply 1 Bottle Trusopt Eye Drops
Instil 2 Drops Tid

Signature Of Mr A Sheep

Practices at: The Gables Anytown, The Parks, Anytown

Partners: Mr A Sheep Veterinary Practitioner, Mr A Lamb MRCVS, Ms A Herd MRCVS

	STATEMENT 1	STATEMENT 2
Question 8.1	The prescription shown is a legal veterinary prescription.	The prescription shown has been signed by a registered veterinary surgeon.
Question 8.2	The prescription shown does not fulfil all the criteria that make it legally valid.	It does not need the statement 'For animal treatment only' on the prescription.

Question 8.3	If a dispensed label for the above preparation was produced, it would be a legal requirement that it should include the name of the animal.	The label for the above prescription would need the name of the owner as a legal requirement.
Question 8.4	Any label for a veterinary product must include the words 'For animal treatment only'.	Any label for a veterinary product must include the words 'Keep out of reach of children'.
Question 8.5	Dispensed labels for human and animal use are exactly the same, except for the addition of the name of the animal.	The additional requirement on a veterinary label is the words 'For animal treatment only'.
Question 8.6	The prescription shown in the figure above is not legally valid.	It is missing the date.

What issues should I consider?

■　In addition to the normal legal requirements for POM prescriptions, record keeping and labels, you will need to consider the extra item(s) needed for veterinary supplies.

Answers and Explanations

Answers and Explanations *8.1*

1　False

The prescription is not legally valid, as it has not been dated.

2　False

At the veterinary practices there are veterinary practitioners and surgeons; they can both issue prescriptions. Mr A. Sheep is a veterinary practitioner, not a surgeon.
　　　Code = E

Answers and Explanations

8.2

1   True

As stated above, the POM requirement for a date is not fulfilled.

2   True

There is no requirement for the words 'For animal treatment only' to be on the prescription.

However, this unnecessary addition does not make the prescription invalid, so statement 2 is not an explanation of statement 1, so:

Code = B

Answers and Explanations

8.3

1   False

The name of the owner is a legal requirement, not that of the animal.

2   True

As stated above.

Code = D

Answers and Explanations

8.4

1   True

This is a legal requirement.

2   True

This is also a legal requirement.

Although both statements are true, statement 2 is not an explanation of statement 1, so:

Code = B

Answers and Explanations

8.5

1   False

A label for a POM veterinary medicine also needs the address of where the animal or herd is kept and the words 'For animal treatment only'. The name of the owner is a legal necessity, not that of the animal.

2   False

As mentioned in statement 1, it legally needs the address of where the animal is kept.

Code = E

Answers and Explanations

8.6

1   True

The point is made again to that a connection between the two statements is necessary for the code to be 'A'.

2   True

Without a date, the prescription is not valid. As statement 2 is an explanation of statement 1:
> Code = A

Question 9

An 'emergency supply at the request of a patient'?

A doctor treated one of his patients for a severe reaction to wasp stings about a year ago. He left the patient with a few of the Piriton injections that he used, in case another doctor needed to treat him as an emergency and did not have a supply. The injections have not been used, but have just gone out of date and the patient is worried that he will be without any until a new supply is obtained.

1   With reference to the conditions for 'emergency supplies at the request of a patient' in the Medicines Act, list all the reasons you can think of as to why you should and should not make the supply.

2   Are there any further considerations that would alter your decision one way or the other? Is there any further information that would help with your decision?

3   What, therefore, is your decision in this case, based on the information given?

What issues should I consider?

- Review the legal requirements discussed in Question 13 at Level 1.
- Use other resources that will assist you in the decision-making process, including the Code of Ethics and the Service specifications.
- To find out more about the process of professional decision-making and the penalties that can be incurred, you will need to study the Level 3 problems, Problems 1 and 2 of which concern emergency supplies.

Answers and Explanations 9

As with so many examples met in real life, the decision as to whether or not to make an 'emergency supply' is not so easy to make as that described at Level 1. The skills of analysing and evaluating are needed – again, just like in practice. Some of the factors you might consider if you were in this position are as follows:

1   Reasons 'against' include:

(a)   It is some time since the last supply?

(b)   There is no 'immediate need' – he has not actually been stung.

(c)   He is not necessarily dependent on that supply, as he is not going to inject himself – the attending doctor could use an alternative.

(d)   The Code of Ethics states that consideration must be made of the medical consequences of not supplying. These might be severe if he is stung and if the attending doctor does not carry an alternative.

(e)   As the patient's supply has only just gone out of date, it could be used, in an emergency.

2   Reasons 'for' include:

(a)   One of your key responsibilities as a pharmacist is to act in the best interests of the patient and to work in partnership with other healthcare professionals.

(b)   The patient has definitely been told to have this medication, not one another doctor might provide.

(c)   The doctor provided a supply for the patient, so that treatment has not been changed.

(d)   If the reaction was bad last time, it is likely to be even more severe if he is stung again – the medical consequences could even be fatal. Would you like to be responsible if he was stung, did not have a supply and had an anaphylactic reaction?

(e)   Chlorphenamine (chlorpheniramine) injections are on the list of POMs that are exempt from the restriction that only a practitioner can give when administered for the purpose of saving life in an emergency.

Other possible influencing factors include:

•   The likelihood of the patient getting stung – the season, his activities, the number of wasps about.

•   How severe his reaction actually was; however, this is not really an area about which you could make a clinical judgement.

•   How soon he could get another prescription and the availability of stock.

You will need to consider your reasons for and against very carefully, and perhaps collect some more information before a decision could be made – you would also want to consider the likely penalties, should the worst happen.

3   On balance, the answer would have to be not to supply, based on the 'lack of an immediate need', but it would be very easy to be persuaded otherwise! Remember you must be able to justify your actions, should the need arise.

Question 10

The legal restrictions imposed on preparations of controlled drugs

This question is designed to be a quick revision exercise of the general Controlled Drugs Regulations, applied to a variety of preparations from the five different Schedules. You will probably find that the best way to approach the problem is to complete as much as you can without referring to any reference sources.

What issues should I consider?

- Be guided by the classification of controlled drugs into five Schedules and the legal restrictions that apply to each under the Misuse of Drugs Act 1971 and the Misuse of Drugs Regulations 1985.

Where should I look in Pharmacy Law & Ethics?

The Misuse of Drugs Act covers all aspects of dealing with controlled drugs; the information you need to complete the table will be found in Chapter 16. You may also need to refer to the *Medicines, Ethics & Practice* guide for the exact legal classification of each preparation.

	Does it have to be stored in the CD cupboard?	Does a CD register entry need to be made?	Does a legal prescription-only register entry need to be made for a private prescription?	Does the destruction of unwanted supplies need to be supervised?	Is export by a community pharmacist allowed?	Does the invoice need to be kept for two years?
Temgesic injections						
Codeine Linctus BP						
Oramorph oral solution						
Tuinal capsules						
Temazepam tablets						
Diazepam tablets						

Answers and Explanations 10	Does it have to be stored in the CD cupboard?	Does a CD register entry need to be made?	Does a legal prescription-only register entry need to be made for a private prescription?	Does the destruction of unwanted supplies need to be supervised?	Is export by a community pharmacist allowed?	Does the invoice need to be kept for two years?
Temgesic injections = Schedule 3 (CD No Reg POM)	Yes – Buprenorphine is an example of the Schedule 3 controlled drugs that need to be in the CD cupboard	No	Yes	No	No	Yes
Codeine Linctus BP = Schedule 5 (CD Inv P)	No	No	No	No	Yes	Yes
Oramorph oral solution = Schedule 5 (CD Inv POM)	No	No	Yes	No	Yes	Yes
Tuinal capsules = Schedule 2 (CD POM)	No – an exception is made for quinalbarbitone; the other ingredient, amylobarbitone is CD No Reg POM	Yes, although most barbiturates are Schedule 3, this is Schedule 2	No – because an entry is made in the CD register, the POR entry would be good practice	Yes	No	No – because an entry is made in the CD register
Temazepam tablets = Schedule 3 (CD No Reg POM)	Yes	No	Yes	No	No	Yes
Diazepam tablets = Schedule 4 Part II (CD Benz POM)	No	No	Yes	No	Yes	No

The Misuse of Drugs Act and the destruction of controlled drugs

The Misuse of Drugs Act 1971 and the Misuse of Drugs Regulations 1985 contain specific requirements about the way in which controlled drugs should be destroyed; other legislation and the Code of Ethics are also pertinent in some instances. In each of the following scenarios, explain what you should do, and which legislation and guidance in the Code of Ethics were used to help you to make your decision.

1   In a routine inspection of stock, you find some morphine injections that have gone out of date. What can be done about them?

2   The widow of a patient who has recently died returns some unused packets of MST tablets and diamorphine injections. Can you take them back into stock and use them for another patient?

3   A drug misuser to whom you supplied methadone mixture under the NHS scheme has recently died. The carers at the hostel where he lived return many empty bottles and some (unused) needles, among which is a small quantity of cannabis. They ask you to re-use the bottles and get rid of everything else for them. Can you help?

What issues should I consider?

■   As in the previous question, you need to consider the Misuse of Drugs Act and the Misuse of Drugs Regulations 1985, this time with respect to the destruction of controlled drugs.

Where should I look in Pharmacy Law & Ethics?

Chapter 16 describes the legal requirements; the environmental issues are covered in Chapter 25. There may be local bye-laws to further complicate the issue.

Answers and Explanations
11

1   As the morphine injections obviously cannot be dispensed or supplied, they must be disposed of. However, they will have been recorded in the appropriate 'CDs received' section of the controlled drugs register but will not have been accounted for in the 'CDs supplied' section. Therefore, if you get rid of the controlled drugs without accounting for them, questions will be asked

by the inspector appointed by the RPSGB and the local police officer, who is usually a member of the drugs squad and referred to as the 'chemist liaison officer'. He or she has the authority to inspect the controlled drugs register on their regular visits. You must therefore wait for one of the persons authorised by the Secretary of State to witness the destruction of the controlled drugs. The person who can act in this capacity may be a member of a class of persons authorised to do so – such as the police officer or pharmaceutical inspector already mentioned. The authorisation also extends to certain pharmacists within large organisations. They will countersign the entry in the controlled drugs register to verify that they have witnessed the destruction. A problem of storage may arise if large quantities of out-of-date controlled drugs accumulate in the controlled drug cupboard; in this case, the chemist liaison officer should be telephoned and asked to call.

There is, however, a further complication in that environmental and local bye-laws may prevent such substances being put into the waste water system. Advice can be sought from the local council; in many instances the chemist liaison officer will take the controlled drugs for destruction in an incinerator, along with other legal and illegal drugs. (In Question 16 at Level 1 the legality of the possession of controlled drugs by a police constable acting in the course of his duty is covered.) Other areas and some large companies issue controlled drugs destruction kits; you need to be aware of the arrangements that apply where you work.

2   Both the Misuse of Drugs Act and the Code of Ethics 3.1 *Practice Guidance* state that if a patient's unused drugs are returned they can be destroyed without any need for the destruction to be witnessed. The fact that the drugs were only recently dispensed and have not been used makes no difference. In the case of controlled drugs, they should not be re-entered into the controlled drug register, but placed in the controlled drug cabinet until they can be destroyed, which should be done as soon as possible, bearing in mind the environmental considerations already mentioned.

3   Most pharmacies receive bottles back, often with the perhaps misguided request to re-use them. Perhaps the best compromise is to recycle the glass containers and, if possible, the plastic parts too.

The needles are unused – which is less of a problem than if they were used. Used needles pose a definite health hazard and a 'sharps' container is needed, together with extreme vigilance on the part of the staff involved; guidance is given to those pharmacists participating in needle exchange schemes (see Service Specifications 20 and 3.1.5 *Practice Guidance*). However, the unused needles could still be a danger if they were thrown out with the ordinary waste; they can be rendered safe by the use of a clipping device, such as those available through the NHS, or by using a health authority needle disposal scheme.

The greatest problem is, however, the cannabis, a Schedule 1 controlled drug that community pharmacists are normally not, under any circumstances, licensed by the Home Office to possess. There are specific exemptions, mainly for hospital pharmacists who may be asked to remove drugs, including illicit drugs, from patients on admission. The carers cannot be authorised to possess and may be in severe difficulties if stopped and found to be in possession. You would probably want to help by taking the controlled drugs from them – and get on the phone fast to the police station to ask for the cannabis to be taken away. You will then be following the practice guidance that is additional to the Code of Ethics service specification 16, namely to work in conjunction with the police when disposing of pharmaceutical waste.

Question

12

Legal requirements for controlled drugs prescriptions

You will need to study the two prescriptions presented below carefully before answering the type 2 MCQs that follow.

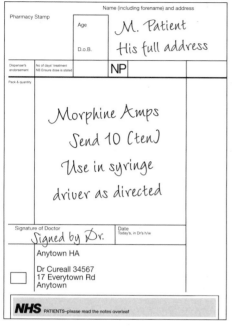

Prescription 1

Prescription 2

Match the statements 1–5 concerning the Misuse of Drugs Act requirements for controlled drugs prescriptions to one of the following answer codes.

A = Prescription 1 only is legally correct – it complies with the all the requirements for prescriptions in the Misuse of Drugs Act and can therefore be supplied.

B = Prescription 2 only is correct (as defined in A).

C = Prescriptions 1 and 2 are both correct (as defined in A).

D = Neither prescription is correct (as defined in A).

E = I am not sure, or would like to qualify my answer.

STATEMENT

1   For controlled drug POM prescriptions, it is essential to have the total quantity of the drug written in both words and figures.

2   For controlled drug POM prescriptions, it is essential to have a dose and a frequency stated.

3   For controlled drug POM prescriptions, it is essential to have the pharmaceutical form stated.

4   For controlled drug POM prescriptions, it is essential to have the name and address of the patient hand-written by the prescriber.

5   For controlled drug POM prescriptions, it is essential to check that the prescriber and the signature are genuine if they are not known to you.

What issues should I consider?

■   Consider whether or not the prescriptions meet the requirements of the Misuse of Drugs Act.

Where should I look in Pharmacy Law & Ethics?

Consult Chapter 16.

Answers and Explanations

12

1   Prescription 1 states the number of dosage units to be dispensed, in words and figures, which is acceptable if there is only one preparation, as the total amount of controlled drug can then be calculated. However, for a preparation such as morphine injections, for which the BNF gives four different strengths, the amount of drug in each ampoule must be stated in order to calculate the total amount to be dispensed.

Prescription 2 tries to conform with the requirement but is incorrect. The prescriber has tried to calculate the total quantity of the drug in five Durogesic '75' patches. However, the '75' refers to the number of mcg that will be released per hour; as the patch is designed to release the drug over 72 hours, the total quantity of the controlled drug fentanyl that it contains is therefore $75 \times 72 = 5400$ mcg. The prescriber could save a lot of trouble by simply writing the number of dosage units – five – in words and figures.

Code = D

2   Prescription 1 does not state a dose or frequency. Even though a nurse is going in to administer the drug through a syringe driver (a device that is used particularly in terminal care to give a patient a continuous infusion of a painkilling drug), and the patient does not need to know how much and how often the drug is to be given, it is a legal requirement that this information is on a controlled drug prescription. The reason for this is to make it a little harder for forgeries to be perpetrated.

Prescription 2 has sufficient information to satisfy the legal requirements for a controlled drug script, but cannot be dispensed until the prescriber has been contacted. The dosage as it is written is very ambiguous and, coupled with the inability to calculate the dose, indicates that the prescriber is not aware of the unusual nature of the dosage form. There is an obvious potential danger to the patient if the instructions were misinterpreted and a new patch applied three times a day or if three were applied at once.

The code is therefore D, or E, on the basis of wanting to clarify the dosage with the prescriber and get it added to the prescription.

3   Both prescriptions 1 and 2 state the pharmaceutical form; this information has to be included, even though it is obvious from the drug name that there is only one dosage form, as in the case of the fentanyl on prescription 2.

Code = C

4   Prescription 1 has the address correctly hand-written by the prescriber.

Prescription 2 has been typed and is not acceptable; it must be returned to the prescriber in order to be rewritten before it can be dispensed.

Code = A

5   The code has to be D or E, as the signature cannot possibly be known in these circumstances. A request for controlled drugs by a prescriber who is unknown to you, especially on a private prescription, might make you think that the prescription is forged. A list of things to look out for that can help detect forgeries is given in the *Practice Guidance* additional to the Code of Ethics.

It is always essential in such circumstances to check that both the prescriber and the signature are genuine.

Question *13*

The sale of Schedule 1 poisons with extra controls: sodium cyanide

Consider the following scenarios.

1   Mr White, whom you know well, is a local pick-your-own fruit grower. He comes into the shop and asks you if he can buy some sodium cyanide to kill wasps' nests that are threatening his business.

(a)   Outline the circumstances that make it permissible for you to make this supply.

(b)   The supply is legal; explain whether or not the following documents are legally necessary:

(i)   a signed order;
(ii)   an entry into the Poisons Register (Schedule 11);
(iii) a 'householder's certificate' (Schedule 10).

2   Mr Black is a local vet who happened to be in the shop when you were serving Mr White; he wants some of the sodium cyanide, as the wasps in the outbuildings at his home are causing problems to his children and the neighbours are complaining.

Explain to Mr Black why you cannot legally sell him the sodium cyanide.

3   As you will not supply the sodium cyanide to Mr Black, he decides to go to Mr White and ask him to exterminate the wasps with a further supply from you.

Can you supply Mr White to treat Mr Black's wasps? Explain the reason(s) for your answer.

4   A commercial firm specialising in the extermination of wasps' nests sets up a business in your area (not surprisingly, in view of the problems that the local residents have). The new manager, Mr Gray, calls into your pharmacy. He wants you to supply his firm with sodium cyanide on a regular basis.

Explain your decision to Mr Gray, together with any conditions that you would have to apply to the requested sale.

What issues should I consider?

■   Review the restrictions on the sale of Schedule 1 poisons.
■   Take into account the extra controls placed upon particularly dangerous substances.

Where should I look in Pharmacy Law & Ethics?

The sale of poisons, including those in Schedule 1, has already been covered in Questions 20–23 at Level 1. Refer to these and also Chapter 17 and Appendix 13 if necessary.

Answers and Explanations

13

1

(a)   The circumstances that permit the supply to Mr White are:

(i)   Sodium cyanide is a Part I, Schedule 1 poison but

is only available under the exemptions that apply in section 4 of Schedule 1. In this case it is exempt because the sale is for use in a trade, business or profession. Clearly, Mr White is in business to make money, not as a hobby, so he would qualify under the section 4 exemption.

(ii) Although the supply is possible under the exemption for a business use, the Schedule 1 restrictions on sale still apply. As you know Mr White, you could be satisfied that he is a person to whom the Schedule 1 poison may properly be sold.

(b) Refer to Question 22 at Level 1 to check on the decision-making process for the sale of a Schedule 1 poison.

(i) As the supply is for business use, he could supply a signed order.

(ii) If Mr White is in the shop in person, he could simply sign the entry in the Poisons Register or, alternatively, the details on the signed order would be entered into the Poisons Register, together with a reference number.

(iii) A 'householder's certificate' (Schedule 10) is not needed, as you know Mr White and do not need a mutual acquaintance (a householder) to vouch for him.

2   The exemptions in section 4 cover business use, among others. Although Mr Black is a vet, the wasps' nests are not at his business premises, but at his home – so the sale is not legally allowed.

3   No, you cannot supply Mr White because his business is growing fruit, not exterminating wasps' nests. Mr White can only purchase the sodium cyanide for his own business use.

4   Unlike the previous scenario, the new firm is in the business, for commercial gain, of exterminating wasps' nests, so it can be supplied with sodium cyanide. However, you do not know Mr Gray – and it is a Schedule 1 poison. He would have to get a householder's certificate (Schedule 10), signed by someone you both knew. If this was not possible, a 'householder' he knows would have to be verified by a police officer, using the second part of the Schedule 10.

Question

14

The Code of Ethics: a preliminary consideration of key and personal responsibilities and other professional standards, service specifications and the additional practice guidance

The key responsibilities are the fundamental, underlying principles of Part 1 of the Code of Ethics, by which the RPSGB (in their capacity as the organisation who regulate the activities of pharmacists) seeks to safeguard and promote the interests of the public and the profession. The key responsibilities should always be considered first when making any decision in the pharmacy. The next consideration is Part 2A, the standards for your personal professional responsibilities, including your professional competence (B) and the need for confidentiality (C). Then you can consider if part 3, the service specifications, contains any guidance about the standards that you, as an individual pharmacist making a professional decision, needs to follow. For example, your preregistration tutor has a specific duty to ensure that section XX of the Society's bye-laws are adhered to.

The service specifications in Part 3 describe both core services and additional services, some of which are supported by practice guidance which is additional advice to that found in the Code of Ethics.

The following questions test your understanding of the Code and the practice advice, where applicable.

Where should I look in Pharmacy Law & Ethics?

In order to help you understand the principles underlying the need for a Code of Ethics and what is meant by the description of pharmacy as a profession, read Chapter 20 and the whole of the revised Code of Ethics before you start trying to answer the questions. Refer to each section as it is mentioned to ensure that you fully understand the implications of the key responsibilities (and, of course, all the other parts of the Code) when it comes to applying the knowledge that you have for the wellbeing and safety of patients.

1   Can you give a medicine to a child aged about eight who comes to collect it for his grandmother who is ill in bed?

2   Is it acceptable to send a member of staff to deliver medicines?

3   When selling vitamins, what can the purchaser be told about the efficacy of the product?

4   You are unable to supply the total quantity of tablets ordered on a prescription and ask the customer to

return for the balance. They ask you to post them. Are you able to do so if the service is requested by the customer?

Answers and Explanations

14

Although the above situations do not at first sight perhaps pose any ethical *problems*, there are several ethical *issues* that need to be considered, and with which the Code will provide some guidance. Here are some of the points you might consider; in each situation, you will see that there is no absolute answer provided by the Medicines Act, for example. Every situation needs to considered on its own, and a professional decision made.

1   As no face-to-face contact will take place between the pharmacist and the patient – as described in Service Specification (SS) 4.1(i) – there is no doubt that there is a need to ensure that SS 8(a) is fully considered. The use of the medicinal product and the necessary advice must be passed on, and the method of delivery must be safe. Your Personal Responsibility (PR) demands that you are accountable, and an understanding of clinical governance means that you need to consider the risks carefully. A phone call may well be an appropriate measure to ensure safe delivery and to pass on advice. Your eventual decision may well depend on the medication, its packaging and the distance the child has to travel.

2   It is possible to delegate duties and send a member of staff when delivering medicines, provided that they are deemed competent – PR A.1(f) – and know that they should refer questions to the pharmacist.

3   The only specific guidance is given in SS 10, in relation to pharmacy medicines, and in SS 12 for complementary therapies. However, the key responsibility regarding truthfulness may help, as the purchaser must not be misled into thinking that the product will have efficacious properties if it will not. Remember that many vitamins are exempt from the Medicines Act, and so preparations do not have to have a marketing authorisation. No claims about what they do apart from their recognised uses can be made, as that would be claiming that they had additional, perhaps unproven, medicinal purposes.

4   SS 4.1(h) gives guidance about incomplete prescriptions, often referred to as 'owings'. As you are keen to

adhere to the key responsibility that guides you to encourage patients to participate in decisions about their care, you may well consider posting the balance an acceptable risk in the circumstances, although the nature of the medication and the risk of it going astray could be significant when making your decision.

You are able to post the balance of a prescription if it is not practicable to supply by other means, providing that certain precautions are taken and that the customer has already been advised as to the use of the medication.

Question

15

The legal and ethical considerations to be made when selling chemicals

A child of about 12 is in the shop. He wants some potassium permanganate to use in his chemistry set. His mother is with him, and assures you that he will be using it under supervision. Do you supply it?

Consider the following points before you reply.

1   Under exactly what circumstances you can legally supply potassium permanganate.

2   How should the package you *might* supply be labelled?

3   Is there any further information that should be provided? Is there any guidance or legislation from other organisations that is applicable or helpful?

4   What responsibility do you have to ensure that the dangers and risks on the container are understood? In other words, are there any ethical points to consider before selling potassium permanganate?

5   If the mother returns and tells you the doctor has told her to purchase some potassium permanganate crystals to mix with water and soak her feet, can you and do you supply it?

What issues should I consider?

Potassium permanganate is a potentially dangerous substance and, if sold to a member of the public, a pharmacist has a responsibility to ensure that it will be used properly.

You will need to check the legal classification of the chemical to ensure it is not a poison or controlled in any way other than under the CHIP regulations.

You also need to consider if there is any guidance in the

Code of Ethics that will help when selling potentially harmful chemicals.

Where should I look in Pharmacy Law & Ethics?

Chapter 18 describes the sale of chemicals that are not poisons or medicinal products but which are controlled under the CHIP regulations.

Answers and Explanations

15

1 Potassium permanganate is not a non-medicinal poison; it can be a medicinal product, but in the first example is a chemical controlled under the CHIP regulations.

Potassium permanganate is classified (by the approved list) as to its category of danger, which according to Appendix 14, describes the general nature of the risk or danger it presents, as:

> physicochemical properties: 'oxidising'
> health effects: harmful

2 The labelling requirements of the CHIP regulations to indicate the general dangers demand that the following symbols are on the label:

The specific information for the particular risks of potassium permanganate is for the words 'Contact with combustible material may cause fire' and 'Harmful if swallowed' to be on the label.

Lastly, the precautions mean that it should also be labelled with the words 'Keep out of reach of children'.

3 In Question 24 at Level 1 we also considered the need to ensure that 'sufficient information' is given to enable the chemical to be used safely. Although the packaging and labelling requirements may be met, additional information can be provided in the form of a safety data sheet; these must be supplied when a chemical is sold for business use, but do not have to be given to private purchasers. The Health and Safety Executive has indicated that sufficient information is more than the standard phrases on the label. Even if a data sheet is available and provided, it is written for business users –

not a 12-year-old. He is unlikely to understand 'oxidising agent' – or the consequences if mixed, however
unlikely, with a reducing agent. On the other hand,
given dire warnings about the explosive nature of the
chemical, a 12-year-old may well be fascinated and
experiment.

4   The Code of Ethics used to have a clear directive that
chemicals, particularly any that could be used to make
fireworks, must not be sold to anyone under 16. The
revised code is much less prescriptive; instead the onus
for acting responsibly in any situation is firmly on the
individual practitioner. In order to consider what that
could mean in this situation, we need to look more
carefully at the key responsibilities and begin to apply
the principles to practice. The example will be just a
taste of the sometimes difficult decision-making process
that is covered in more detail at Level 3.

Let's take the key responsibilities in order:

> 'Acting in the interests of patients and other mem-
> bers of the public, and seek to provide the best
> possible healthcare . . .'

You might think that because the chemical is not a
medicinal product being used to relieve the symptoms
of an illness, the underlying philosophy doesn't apply –
wrong. Without even beginning to question the meaning of the word 'healthcare' and how wide that might
be, there is another very general phrase that applies to
all the key responsibilities, namely that 'Pharmacists in
professional practice use their knowledge for the wellbeing and safety of patients and the public'.

In case your level of responsibility is still not too
clear, have a look at the next key responsibility:

> 'pharmacists must ensure that their knowledge
> . . . is up to date.'

So even if your days of A-level chemistry and university
'practicals' are but a distant memory, you still have an
obligation to be aware of what the dangers of the
chemical you are selling (a professional service) actually
mean. It is no different to the need, as a responsible
professional, to undertake some personal development
to learn about the side-effects of new drugs that you
dispense. Furthermore, without wishing to labour the
point too much, you, as a pharmacist with the indi-

vidual responsibility to provide professional services, are also accountable for your decisions. Again, the exercises in Level 3 discuss in far more detail the implications of being accountable, especially in the light of clinical governance and risk management considerations.

> 'Pharmacists must ensure that they behave with integrity and probity.'

These words are probably not ones that you use every day, and for many their dictionary definition may not be known. A brief examination of both terms will reveal references to truthfulness, honesty, wholeness and adherence to moral principles, which fits in nicely with the definition of ethics; their interpretation in the present context then becomes very clear. The importance of their inclusion in connection with the need for professional standards and levels of behaviour do not need to be discussed any further – it's simply what is expected of you as a pharmacist at all times.

Before you make your decision whether or not to sell, you will also need to think about the term a 'duty of care' and further words from Part 1 of the Code of Ethics:

> 'when faced with ethical dilemmas, pharmacists are expected to use their professional judgement in deciding on the most appropriate course of action. They must be able to justify their action to their peers . . .'

How would you feel if he did experiment and harmed himself and/or others? What would your liability be in this situation? We have already decided that you are accountable for your actions.

It is probably best to refuse the sale and discuss with the boy and his mother the possibility of some supervised lessons rather than experimentation at home.

5   The supply to the mother is for a medicinal product, and would appear to be totally legal and ethical. Perhaps the obligatory wording for potassium permanganate as both a medicinal product and as a chemical – 'keep out of reach of children' – provides a useful guide to your actions.

Question 16

The Code of Ethics and additional guidance: the provision of professional services

The following statements, in the form of type 4 MCQs, concern the provision of professional services from community pharmacies and the advice that is given by the RPSGB to assist pharmacists.

	STATEMENT 1	STATEMENT 2
Question 16.1	Any pharmacist who offers to provide a domiciliary pharmaceutical service for a nursing or residential home must complete the education pack 'The home away from home' before providing the service.	Any pharmacist who visits a nursing or residential home must make his or her own arrangements with the patient and does not need to involve any outside agencies.
Question 16.2	Any pharmacist offering a service to a residential home must undertake to train the care staff at the home.	Any pharmacist offering a service to a residential home needs to consider the number of residents that are to be included in the service.
Question 16.3	Any pharmacist offering a delivery service to a housebound customer must receive the prescription from the doctor within 72 hours of the doctor's telephoned request.	Any prescription delivery service from the community pharmacy should include a requirement for the recipient to sign that they have received the medication.
Question 16.4	Pharmacists should take part in any local health promotion activities and initiatives such as 'No Smoking day'.	Pharmacists could use the information they need to help with 'No Smoking day' from the manufacturer's literature for nicotine replacement therapy.
Question 16.5	When providing a service to drug misusers, the pharmacist is able to draw up a contract with a client regarding the time of day that the prescription can be collected.	A pharmacist can pre-empt any trouble that the provision of a methadone supervision service might cause at busy times by asking - even insisting - that drug misusers leave their dogs outside.

■ Think about what is meant by a professional service
and how pharmacists can provide such facilities to the
benefit of the community, their patients and their own
job satisfaction by using the specialist advice and
resources available to them.

In addition to the consideration of key responsibilities and
accountability in Part 1, consider the *Practice Guidance* (Part
3, numbered as 3.1.1 etc.) that accompanies the Code of
Ethics, Part 2: *Standards and Service Specifications* (SS).

**Answers
and
Explanations**

16

**Answers
and
Explanations**

16.1

1   False

3.1.2 Pharmacists are advised to complete the education
pack, but it is not mandatory.

2   False

Any pharmacist who visits a nursing or residential home is
advised to liaise with outside agencies such as the social
services department before a contract is agreed between the
pharmacist and the local commissioning authority.
    Code = E

**Answers
and
Explanations**

16.2

1   False

A pharmacist can provide training, but does not have to. At
the time the pharmacist agrees to provide a service to the
home, a contract is agreed with the health authority, which
may include training.

2   True

Apart from the directive in 3.1.2 to negotiate a contract as to
the number of homes to be included in the service, it would
be appropriate, in view of the personal responsibility to only
accept work for which they have the requisite skills and
facilities. There is also perhaps the need to mention the
requirement to provide a reasonably prompt service – SS 4.1
and 8.
    Code = D

Answers and Explanations

16.3

1   True

As with any 'emergency supply at the request of the doctor', the doctor has 72 hours in which to send you the prescription.

2   True

See SS 8(c) regarding the audit trail and signature requirement.
    Code = B, as the two true statements are not connected.

Answers and Explanations

16.4

1   True

See SS 13. Pharmacists are encouraged to participate in any local and national health promotion schemes.

2   False

There is a lot more information available, from local and national sources; care should be taken to ensure that the information is not compromised by commercial considerations (b).
    Code = C

Answers and Explanations

16.5

1   True

SS 19(c) allows the pharmacist to anticipate the problems that might be experienced by detailing the expectations of the service from both the user's and the pharmacist's viewpoint. Just because the user is collecting methadone under the NHS instalment scheme, it does not mean that the key responsibilities do not apply. Read the key responsibilities again and you will realise that the drug misuser has just as much right to expect the best possible healthcare etc. Such concepts are part of the Code of Ethics, and it's possible that you will need to find out more as you begin to understand some of the issues that are raised in connection with potentially difficult areas of practice. Read more about prioritising and ascribing values in Level 3.

2   True

Again, this is beginning to apply what the Code means to real examples of dilemmas that happen in practice. Go back to key responsibility 1 and think about the other members of the public that you will be trying to serve – mothers with pushchairs and frail old ladies perhaps. Then think about

your liability and accountability in the case of an accident –
and the risks involved. There's no easy answer; it is your
personal responsibility to decide!

Question

17

The Code of Ethics: the sale of substances liable to abuse

As a pharmacist you will be expected to supply a wide variety
of substances that have the potential to be misused. The
following type 4 MCQs test your knowledge of the advice
issued by the RPSGB to help you to fulfil your obligations in
this respect.

	STATEMENT 1	STATEMENT 2
Question **17.1**	It would be illegal for a pharmacist to offer for sale a substance that claims to speed up the elimination of alcohol from the body, even it were not specifically mentioned in the guidance on substances of misuse.	Although there are explicit statements regarding some medicinal products and their misuse, these are not exhaustive.
Question **17.2**	A definitive list of the substances liable to misuse is published in the *Medicines, Ethics & Practice* guide.	The drugs that are especially likely to be abused include the controlled drug Diconal.
Question **17.3**	One of the things that may make a pharmacist suspicious about the possibility of a forged prescription is the use of unusual methods to produce headed notepaper for 'private' prescriptions.	Every pharmacist must be vigilant as to the possibility that a prescription from an unknown prescriber may be forged.

What issues should I consider?

- You will need to think about the substances that have the potential to be misused, together with any of the relevant reasons for abuse that could be influential in predicting new possibilities.
- You will also need to be aware of the possible signs that a person is misusing legal and illegal substances, and the ways by which he or she might seek to obtain supplies.

Where should I look in Pharmacy Law & Ethics?

There is no one reference that is going to give all the answers to the questions being raised; indeed, some of the issues may not have a single correct response. What you will need to do is consider many of the principles in the Code of Ethics as a starting point to help you decide how you, as a professional, will be expected to act. Some specific sources of help are given in the answers, but in many instances you will need to approach the problems in the same manner as for the Level 3 questions. The pharmacists' Code of Ethics includes a statement to the effect that 'pharmacists are expected to use their professional judgement in deciding on the most appropriate course of action'. Perhaps it is now time to move onto Level 3 to find out more!

Answers and Explanations

17

Answers and Explanations

17.1

1   True

Although many well-known substances are mentioned, there is also a requirement that every pharmacist must be aware of other, perhaps local, problems too.

2   True

It is perhaps difficult to state that such a substance is actually being misused in the conventional sense; it is more appropriate to say that there is potential, and that you have the key responsibility to act with integrity.
Statement 2 is therefore an explanation of statement 1, so
Code = A

Answers and Explanations

17.2

1   False

A section on substances liable to abuse is published in the miscellaneous Practice Advice, but the list it contains is not exhaustive or definitive; other preparations may well be involved, at both local and national levels.

2   True

You will need to consult the list mentioned above, in which Diconal is mentioned as a controlled drug particularly liable to abuse.
Code = D

Answers
and
Explanations

17.3

1   False

In the same section (3.4.4) on substances of misuse, a list of some of the things that should alert a pharmacist to the possibility of a forged prescription is given; unusual headed notepaper is not listed.

2   True

The possibility that an unknown prescriber has issued a forged prescription must always be considered; there are several other factors that would need to be taken into account.

Code = D

Introduction to Questions 18–20

The last section of questions at Level 2, i.e. Questions 18–20, is set to cover some aspects of the law listed in the registration examination syllabus that have not already been included in the preceding questions. Some of the material to be examined is beyond the scope of Dale and Appelbe's *Pharmacy Law and Ethics*; also, the legislation on which much of the material is set is continually being revised and updated. Consequently, there are frequent alterations. In order to keep abreast of such changes, it is necessary to refer to the following additional reference sources:

- material sent to preregistration graduates by the RPSGB, or available on the designated section of the website (www.rpsgb.org.uk). This would include the registration exam syllabus;
- information sent throughout the year to preregistration graduates and their tutors (often in the form of a bulletin);
- articles published in the *Pharmaceutical Journal* to enable practising pharmacists to keep up to date;
- literature produced by individual companies and organisations, such as the National Pharmaceutical Association (NPA) and the multiple community pharmacy employers, who have a responsibility for a number of preregistration trainees.

It is emphasised that the above resources should be consulted in addition to the references given in the questions.

The 'tenets' of Clinical Governance

As an NHS organisation, community pharmacy has to be seen to be incorporating Clinical Governance into the services it provides to the NHS. The best known definition of Clinical Governance refers to a framework through which continuous quality improvement of clinical care may be delivered. In the introduction to Level 3, there is further guidance and interpretations as to what it means in practice. The questions that are set here are based on what are called the 'tenets' of Clinical Governance at the end of Part 2 of the Code of Ethics, in which personal responsibilities and the need to follow the 'tenets' whenever a professional service is provided are described.

In order to consider what the 'tenets' mean in practice, some examples of professional services are given; you are then expected to select one of the codes A–E which describe possible priorities in that situation. It is accepted that you will probably find selecting just one very difficult; try to justify your particular reasons before referring to the author's suggestions.

The questions are also examples of the registration exam requirement for questions to be set that test the key skills of analysis and evaluation.

STATEMENT

A   An identifiable pharmacist is accountable for all activities undertaken.

B   All pharmacists and their staff are suitably trained and competent to perform the tasks required.

C   Any necessary equipment and facilities are available for the provision of the service and that these are maintained in good order.

D   Risk assessment and management procedures have been identified and are followed.

E   Adequate records are maintained to enable the service to be monitored.

1   You have agreed with the local health authority (or its equivalent) to offer a blood cholesterol testing service under a Patient Group Directive to every customer with a prescription for a 'statin'. The referral levels and other aspects of the service have been discussed and agreed with the local GPs. You are now at the stage of deciding which machine to use, and who will perform the tests.

2   A customer brings back a prescription which she says has been dispensed wrongly; on investigation, you find

that she should have had a pack of Amiloride tablets but was given amlodipine. After redispensing the item correctly and apologising to the customer, you discuss with your dispenser how the same mistake can be avoided in the future.

3   An unknown customer says they have run out of their medication; after a lengthy consultation, you decide that you cannot do an emergency supply as they do not have sufficient evidence as to their exact prescription.

4   You are asked to do a locum duty in a very busy pharmacy with lots of prescriptions to be assembled for the local nursing home. You ask if a trained dispensing assistant will be on duty to assist you.

5   One of the regular drug misusers is in the shop wanting their methadone to be dispensed now, if not sooner. The prescription is not due until tomorrow, which is explained very clearly to them, and you explain that you will not break the law on their behalf. They complain to the clinic, who are surprised and disappointed that you will not help your patient in an emergency.

Answers and Explanations

18

1   If the Patient Group Directive has been agreed, the proposed service must already have met various quality criteria, including the issue of accountability (A) and the risks inherent in taking blood samples and how they will be managed (D). As the machine and the service is not yet available, C and E do not apply. The answer is B; the consideration of the machine and which member of staff should be used must include the need for, and provision of, adequate training to use the machine properly, so that the results are accurate and reliable.

2   The question of accountability (A) is not in question here – it is always the pharmacist on duty at the time the error was made. It is probably not training, (B), assuming that the dispenser has undergone a recognised course and is not just someone from the shop 'helping' out. It is possibly the facilities if there is not adequate space or if the dispensary is too small, but all those issues should be encompassed in managing the risks of running a pharmacy. If there is a reliance on under-trained staff working accurately in too small a space that is perhaps untidy or badly organised, errors are likely to happen – and it is not too difficult to see who has the responsibility to prevent them as far as is

possible. Similarly packaged 'generic' patient packs have been blamed for a lot of recent problems, but there are other reasons too. Remember the key responsibility for the wellbeing and safety of patient? Clinical Governance helps put that into action; a key factor in improving quality is managing risks appropriately (D).

3   The Medicines Act gives the legal requirements that must be followed if a supply is to be made, and the Code of Ethics demands that you consider the consequences of not supplying, as we have already seen. Further issues of the difficulties of making such a decision are examined at Level 3. Here all the questions have been answered and the decision made; all that you need to do now, just in case there are further questions asked by a doctor, for example, is to keep adequate records of what you did and exactly why you made that decision, even though in this instance it was not to supply. Answer = (E).

4   When you are asked to do a locum, it is expected that you will ask questions about the numbers of prescriptions, when the items are required for, the systems in use and the level of support staff needed. However, the Code of Ethics now makes it very clear that you have a responsibility not to take on work for which you are not competent, or for which there is inadequate provision of facilities and equipment, so although every aspect of Clinical Governance is relevant, (C) is the overriding concern in this instance.

5   Although you might not think so, this question is the easiest of all the situations. In previous exercises we have discussed all the key and professional responsibilities and considered how they might apply to different patients – or not, as the case may be. We have also thought about all the extra guidance that applies to particular professional services. You might even have referred to SS 19 concerning the standards expected when offering a service to drug misusers. However relevant and useful that may be, it does not apply here; nothing changes the law – in this case the Misuse of Drugs Act. You, the pharmacist in charge, are accountable for your actions and will bear the consequences of breaking the law, however well intentioned. Consequently answer (A) applies. Where the Code of Ethics does help is to make you think of the consequences of your actions and where your responsibilities lie – to help your patient.

If you have found these problems difficult, that's only to be expected; the main aim of the preregistration year is prepare you for practice as an independent and effective professional. It's definitely time to look at Level 3 in order to find out more about how to make professional decisions.

Question 19

Miscellaneous legislation affecting pharmacy: the Data Protection Act 1998

The Data Protection Act is another example of the miscellaneous legislation that affects community pharmacists; your knowledge of the Act is tested below. Note that the exam guidance does not require a detailed knowledge of the legislation, but does require the ability to demonstrate an understanding of how the Act applies to the relevant aspects of practice.

1 The Data Protection Act has its own terminology. Four of the terms are listed below, together with a description (not in the correct order) of what each one means. Match each of the terms and their correct description.
   Data Protection Act terminology:

(a) data processor;
(b) personal data;
(c) data subject;
(d) processed.

   Description of the terms:

   (i) the person to whom the data relates;
   (ii) any information whereby a living individual can be identified;
   (iii) anyone who processes the data, apart from the data controller;
   (iv) virtually any activity to do with the use of data, which can be computerised or held in any other storage system that can retrieve data relating to a living person.

2 State the eight Data Protection principles.
3 Pharmacists are controlled by the Act when they keep computerised patient medication records, and so they need to think of the implications regarding their personal responsibility to respect and maintain confiden-

tiality. Try to answer the following questions with the PR 2.C in mind.

(a)   What has to be done by a member of the public who wants to gain access to his or her patient medication record?

(b)   What can be done by a pharmacist who does not want to provide the data?

(c)   If a person other than the data subject asks for a copy of their PMR, what options does the pharmacist have?

Where should I look in Pharmacy Law & Ethics? — Read Chapter 25 on the miscellaneous legislation that affects pharmacy, including what is controlled by the Data Protection Act and how it may affect the way in which a community pharmacy is organised and run.

Answers and Explanations

19

1

Data Protection Act terminology	*Number and description of term*
(a) Data processor	(iii) Anyone who processes the data, apart from the data controller
(b) Personal data	(ii) Any information whereby a living individual can be identified
(c) Data subject	(i) The person to whom the data relates
(d) Processed	(iv) Virtually any activity to do with the use of data, which can be computerised or held in any other storage system that can retrieve data relating to a living person

2   Very briefly, the eight Data Protection principles are as follows:

Data must:

(a)   be obtained fairly and lawfully;

(b)   be obtained and processed only for a specific and lawful purpose;

(c)   be adequate, relevant and not excessive;

(d)   be accurate and kept up to date;

(e)   be kept for no longer than necessary;

(f)   processed in accordance with the rights of data subjects;

(g)   be protected against unauthorised or unlawful processing etc.;

(h)   not be transferred outside the European Economic Area.

3

(a) The data subject can apply in writing to the data controller, paying a fee.

(b) The first essential step is to ensure that it is the data subject (or a healthcare professional under the terms of the Act) making the request. If the controller (in this case the pharmacist) did not want to disclose the data – perhaps because he or she thought it might cause distress – the detailed exemptions would have to be consulted.

(c) The pharmacist needs to read carefully their PR regarding the confidentiality of information before deciding whether or not it is possible to disclose such information without consent. It would also be appropriate to consider the Access to Health Records Act 1990, although most of the legislation concerning living persons is now enclosed in the Data Protection Act.

What further issues should I consider?

The very real difficulties that a pharmacist may encounter, and the possible consequences if information is not disclosed, are dealt with in Problem 13 at Level 3.

Question

20

Miscellaneous legislation affecting pharmacy: the Health and Safety at Work etc. Act 1974

Pharmacists who act as employers and superintendents have additional personal responsibilities which involve protecting their staff and the public. The provisions of the Health and Safety at Work Act cover some of their responsibilities in this area, which are dealt with in the following questions. Pre-registration trainees are not expected to have anything other than a basic understanding of such legislation.

1 Name the two groups of people covered by the Act, giving examples where appropriate.

2 Give five duties of employers with respect to the Act in order to ensure the health, safety and welfare of their employees.

3 Outline two duties of the Health and Safety Executive under the Act.

4 Outline four duties of the Heath and Safety Commission under the Act.

Think about what is controlled by the Health and Safety at Work Act and how this may affect the way in which a community pharmacy is organised and run.

**Answers
and
Explanations**

20

1

(a)   Persons at work – employers, employees and the self-employed.

(b)   The public.

2

(a)   To provide adequate maintenance of plant and systems of work so that they are reasonably safe and free from risk.

(b)   To ensure the safe use, handling and storage and transport of articles and substances.

(c)   To provide instruction, training and supervision to ensure health and safety.

(d)   If there are more than five employees, to provide a written statement of policy with regard to health and safety.

(e)   To conduct the business in such a way that members of the public are not exposed to a risk to health and safety.

3

(a)   To carry out duties as directed by the Health and Safety Commission.

(b)   As an enforcement body it can appoint inspectors who can deal with breaches of the Act.

4

(a)   The Health and Safety Commission is responsible to the Secretary of State to make arrangements for health and safety.

(b)   It is responsible for shops, offices and factories, but not agriculture.

(c)   It is responsible for the provision of information, advice and research about the Act.

(d)   It can arrange for other government departments to exercise some functions on its behalf.

3

Level Three

Introduction to Level 3 problems

We use several terms in the next section that may need some explanation. These are mainly to do with the kinds of law that apply to pharmacy practice. Although it is an oversimplification, it is helpful to classify these with reference to the sanction or penalty which may follow a breach of each kind of law.

Thus, society requires breaches of *criminal law* to be followed by prosecution and a penalty, such as prison or a fine. Specific offences are created under criminal law, and an enforcement authority, usually the police, is appointed. Examples in the area of pharmacy are prosecution by the police, probably the local drug squad officer, for failure to maintain the controlled drugs register, which is a breach of the Misuse of Drugs Act. Similarly, for many offences created under the Medicines Act, such as failure to supervise the sale of a pharmacy (P) medicine, the Royal Pharmaceutical Society is the enforcement authority and can bring its own prosecutions to court (Chapter 19).

Other parliamentary legislation creates a division of criminal law called *administrative law*, which gives power to public bodies to regulate certain activities. The NHS 'Terms of Service' are an example (Chapter 23). The sanctions for a breach of Terms of Service are administered through the local health body's disciplinary process, which includes power to 'withhold remuneration' or ultimately to disqualify a pharmacy contractor from holding an NHS contract. Whereas a fine under criminal law is paid to the courts and reverts to the treasury, a withholding will be retained by the health body which has power to administer NHS contracts.

In the hospital and primary care service, the Department of Health has power to discipline and fine NHS and Primary Care Trusts which fail to meet the 'statutory duty of quality'. This is defined in the Health Act 1999 as 'a duty to put and keep in place arrangements for the purpose of monitoring and improving the quality of health care which it provides to individuals' and is usually referred to as 'clinical governance' (Chapters 20 and 23). Clinical governance requires attention to the clinical quality of the care being given – such as ensuring that there is a good evidence base for the selection of medicines prescribed for a particular condition – and to the operational quality of the service itself – safeguarded through risk management, including risk assessment, the setting of standards, use of standard operating procedures, audit mechanisms and review. It is this second aspect of clinical governance which is relevant to the legal and ethical issues raised in the problems which follow.

Guidance on what standards should apply is regularly issued in a range of ways, such as Health Service Circulars, National Service Frameworks and Controls Assurance requirements. All of these approximate to mandatory standards in that failure to implement them without good reason could result in financial penalties for the NHS body and would be a source of censure in the event of civil litigation (see below). It is also likely that staff and managers who failed to implement adequate clinical governance arrangements would find their continued employment in jeopardy.

You should also note that although clinical governance is not yet statutorily applicable to the activities of community pharmacists, unless those activities are part of an NHS contract, the principles are implicit in the key responsibilities of a pharmacist and are explicitly required in the preamble to the service specifications which are appended to the Code.

Civil law provides remedies for breach of *common law* duties owed by individuals to one another. This is a separate branch of law with a system of courts distinct from those used for criminal law. Breaches of common law duties can lead to a civil action by the injured party (claimant) against another (respondent) for compensation. The most likely area for pharmacists to become involved in a civil action is negligence (Chapter 20). When a customer comes to a pharmacist for a service or advice, the pharmacist has a 'duty of care' to that customer, i.e. to act responsibly, competently and professionally. If the pharmacist fails in some way and that failure results in 'damage' or injury to the customer, then the customer might be able to claim compensation from the pharmacist for negligence.

Other common law duties that could arise in practice include a duty to maintain confidentiality over patient information and to be discreet in discussions about patients to avoid 'defamation'. Suppose that a pharmacist knew that an unmarried woman had had a positive pregnancy test and then gossiped, with inappropriate rude remarks, about this to other staff or customers in the shop. The woman might then have a claim against the pharmacist for breach of confidence and for making defamatory remarks about her that tended to lower her standing in the eyes of others.

We also talk about *vicarious liability* (Chapter 25) which, in this context, means the responsibility assumed by employers for the actions of their employees and their consequences. If you are not an employee, perhaps working as a locum or freelance consultant, then you should ensure that you are covered by liability insurance to cover any claims made against you (see also the Code of Ethics, Chapter 20).

Finally, we refer to the concept of 'taking all reasonable steps' (sometimes called 'due diligence') as a defence, which recognises that, although it is not always possible to be absolutely certain about every aspect of a problem, you should be 'reasonably certain'. Suppose that you receive a phone call from someone who says that she is the pharmacist at a hospital and that there is an unconscious patient in casualty who appears to have taken a drug overdose. The patient has a medication record card from your pharmacy in his wallet – will you tell the pharmacist what medication he is taking?

Before giving this information you must take 'all reasonable steps' to establish that the call is genuine. You do not know from a phone call who is at the other end. If you are given a return phone number you do not know if this is genuine without checking. So you might obtain the number of the hospital from an independent source, perhaps directory inquiries, and then phone to check that someone of the name you have been given is working there.

Such tactics are not foolproof, but they are 'reasonable' in the circumstances and show that you are discharging your duty to care enough about patient confidentiality not to disclose details to casual callers, who might just be from the local newspaper!

Professional decision-making

As a professional and a pharmacist, you must often exercise professional judgement based on your experience and assessment of the consequences of a range of decisions. In achieving this, a rapid application of knowledge from many different areas is necessary to reach a judgement as to what is right for the patient and is achievable in a given set of circumstances.

Take two real life examples (*Pharm J* 23 March 1991 p.371 and *Pharm J* 21 November 1991 p.608):

> Two pharmacists were reprimanded by the Statutory Committee in 1991 following convictions for the supply to a 17-year-old youth of sodium cyanide in one case and strychnine hydrochloride, potassium permanganate and glycerol in another.

Why were such supplies considered wrong? What thought processes should have been gone through in reaching a decision as to whether to supply? Pharmacists are permitted to supply all these substances from a pharmacy, so why were convictions as well as a reprimand given? Would it have been right to supply in other circumstances? If so, on what knowledge would you have based your decision?

What is needed before any decision can be taken is as many facts as possible. We shall call this:

Stage 1: gather relevant facts

1   What criminal law applies here?

First, you will want to know what the criminal law says. Ask yourself 'will I be breaking the law if I supply?' In the case of potassium permanganate you may supply, but there are packaging and labelling regulations to consider (Chapter 18). You may supply glycerol; indeed, you can buy glycerol (or glycerin) from the food shelves of a supermarket. Neither of these substances is controlled as a medicine or a poison. Sodium cyanide and strychnine are both Part I, Schedule 1, poisons with special conditions attaching to their supply (Chapter 19). Most of the criminal law that applies to pharmacy practice will be in the Medicines Act, the Misuse of Drugs Act or the Poisons Act, although there is a whole range of other criminal legislation (Chapter 25) that may apply, for example, the Environmental Protection Act 1990, the Health and Safety at Work etc. Act 1974, the Customs and Excise Management Act 1979.

2   What NHS law applies here?

In this example, you do not have to consider NHS law because the supply is a 'private' one and not within the terms of the NHS contract. There are other aspects of administrative law, such as employment protection, which will apply to pharmacy practice, but in these examples we mostly consider NHS law, specifically the Terms of Service requirements and clinical governance.

3   What civil law applies here?

In this example, the young man managed to cause an explosion by using glycerol and potassium permanganate together. Would the supplying pharmacist have been partly to blame for any damage that may have resulted? To some extent, yes, because pharmacists are expected, by virtue of their expertise and training, to exercise a greater *duty of care* than other retailers over the supplies they make. In the case of strychnine and cyanide, sales are restricted to pharmacies precisely because pharmacists are expected to know the dangers inherent in their use and only to supply responsibly after due enquiries have been made. The areas of civil law that are most likely to be an issue in pharmacy practice are negligence, confidentiality and defamation.

4   What guidance does the Code of Ethics give here?

As a pharmacist, you have to meet standards that are in excess of the minimum that the law requires. At the time of this case, the Code of Ethics said 'A pharmacist must take steps to ensure that all chemicals supplied will be used for a proper purpose and in appropriate circumstances'. The Code went on to give guidance that all oxidising agents, such as potassium permanganate, may be used for the preparation of explosives. (Such requirements are now implicit in the legal requirement to exercise 'due diligence' when supplying any chemicals.) What enquiries should you make? What facts will you need to show that you made reasonable enquiries to satisfy these requirements?

5 What professional knowledge do I have which applies here?

Notwithstanding all the legal and ethical constraints or guidance that you are aware of, you will also be applying your technical and clinical knowledge to the situation. You probably learned in chemistry classes that certain chemicals make explosive combinations. You would know that cyanide and strychnine are immensely potent poisons. Do you think it would be safe to supply to a 17-year-old? Many of the problems you encounter in pharmacy practice will require the use of your knowledge of therapeutics, pharmaceutics, good pharmacy practice etc., as well as knowledge of law and ethics.

6 Where can I look or who can I ask for help?

Finally, but just as important as any of the above, is whether there is any precedent you can follow, any policy that covers this situation, any other 'rule book' or senior pharmacist that perhaps you should consult. Many pharmacists are employees who will have corporate protocols and procedures to follow and, most valuable at the start of a career, a range of experienced pharmacists who can be asked for advice. Delaying action to take advice is always an option to consider.

When you have the answers to these questions or you decide that they do not apply, then you will have assembled the raw material from which to make your decision. Increasingly, pharmacists may expect to be challenged on their assembly of facts: what questions were asked, what was the condition of the patient, what possibilities were excluded etc. Good practice usually demands that records should be made at the time to demonstrate a conscientious and informed approach and justify the ultimate decision taken.

Stage 2: prioritise and ascribe values

When you have all the information that you can get, you will find that some facts are going to be more important than others. In this example, the fact that the purchaser in the above example is male is interesting but not important; his age, however, may influence your eventual decision. Even if the purchaser were a middle-aged, respectable-looking individual, you might still consider the nature of the substances or combination of substances to be of overriding importance. You are prioritising the facts.

Moreover, you will want to weigh up the consequences for yourself, perhaps for your employer, for the young man, for his parents and neighbours and for the reputation of pharmacy of making these supplies or not. The relative importance you attach to these issues will also depend on your own personal opinions and attitudes. In other words, you are ascribing values to the facts you have assembled.

There will be a whole range of individuals and affected parties whose interests you should consider.

1   First, you will want to promote the health and welfare or at least cause no harm to the *patient*, or, in this case, the *purchaser*.

2   The interests of other players in the example must also be considered. What would be the consequences to the *patient's carer*, *parents* or *relatives*? In this case, *neighbours*, or even *perfect strangers*, might have suffered serious harm from the sale of potential explosives or poisons to this young man. Or you may have information about an HIV-positive individual that might raise in your mind questions about the interests of the patient as compared with those of other people who were *sexual contacts*.

3   You have a duty as a pharmacist to uphold the reputation of the pharmacy profession (a key responsibility of a pharmacist in the Code of Ethics). This means that you should do nothing to undermine confidence in you as an *individual pharmacist* and as a *representative of the profession* to which you belong.

4   You also have a duty to co-operate with *healthcare professionals* and others for the benefit of *patients* and the *public* (another key responsibility in the Code of Ethics). Some later examples show how you may have to weigh your obligation, or that of your staff, to preserve the patient's faith in the doctor against the potential risk of harm to the patient.

5   If you are employed, your *employer* carries liability for what you do in the course of your employment – 'vicarious liability' (Chapter 25). This liability is not limitless; if you fail to follow your employer's instructions or the terms of your employment contract then you may be held accountable for your actions. In most situations you will also have a duty to maintain other people's confidence in your employers in the same way as you represent your profession.

6   Finally, you will have your own set of moral and cultural values which create obligations to *yourself*. Again, some later examples may show how attitudes and moral convictions may be the overriding consideration for some individuals, although the Code of Ethics (personal responsibilities for pharmacists providing professional services) makes it clear that such matters must not be allowed to compromise your first priority – the welfare of the patient.

So, how can we summarise this stage? Decide what priority and value you attach to the interests of the following:

- the patient or customer;
- those near to the patient – parents, carers, dependants;
- those in contact with the patient – neighbours, contacts, the public at large;
- your own profession and other professionals with whom you work;
- your employer and work colleagues;
- yourself.

Good pharmacy practice requires that you balance the disparate interests of all the parties concerned and are prepared to record where necessary and justify the reasoning that led to your eventual decision. This means that you will move onto the next stage automatically.

Stage 3: generate options

In other words, ask yourself: 'What *could* I do in this situation?'
In this example there will be at least four options:

1   supply none of the items;
2   supply all of the items;
3   supply some of the items;
4   delay to seek advice.

You might suggest other variations such as selling some or all of the items subject to certain conditions, such as a written request specifying reason for purchase or giving the authority of someone you know to be responsible. By careful analysis, you will be able to establish the likely consequences of each course of action and then choose which will have the best chance of a good outcome or, in some cases, the least likelihood of causing harm.

You are now ready to move to the final stage.

Stage 4: choose an option

In other words ask yourself: 'What *should* I do in this situation?'

Remember that, when making your choice, you may have to be able to justify why you made that one. This is not as daunting as it may seem as you will be able to draw on many sources of help to reach your decision, such as your reference books and manuals, your colleagues, your employer or your professional and trade body. Gradually you will add to this your own experience, your knowledge of real life, perhaps your knowledge of the purchaser (or in other cases patients and their families) or the local environment in which you are practising pharmacy. The whole process develops your professional judgement, which distinguishes the professional from the technician and indicates an ability to respond to unfamiliar and unexpected situations that fall outside the rule book.

When you first looked at the example used, you almost certainly made a rapid decision that you would not have made these supplies of sodium cyanide, strychnine, potassium permanganate and glycerol. We would suggest that this is the correct option. But in reaching it you unconsciously and very quickly ran through your technical and legal knowledge, assessed the purchaser, considered the consequences of supplying or not and what options you had and then chose not to supply. It probably took you less than a minute to decide, although it might take a little longer to decide how you would explain your decision to the would-be purchaser!

Another way of structuring the decision-making process in more complex areas is to hypothesise–test–reject and repeat the process until you are left with one hypothesis that meets all your tests. This is the standard problem-solving process you have used many times to make reasoned judgements about problems you have had to face.

Summary

1 **Gather relevant facts**	What applies here? ■ criminal, NHS and civil law; ■ the Code of Ethics; ■ Council statements; ■ professional and other knowledge.
2 **Prioritise and ascribe values**	What are the interests of: ■ the patient; ■ the public; ■ carers; ■ relatives and neighbours; ■ other healthcare professionals; ■ the pharmacy profession; ■ your employer; ■ yourself?
3 **Generate options** What *could* you do?	■ What are the possible consequences of each option? ■ How likely are the consequences?
4 **Choose an option** What *should* you do?	■ Can you justify the chosen option?

How to work through the problems

Each of the following problems describes a situation that calls for you to apply your legal and ethical, and other, knowledge of pharmacy practice to provide a solution. The complexity and the breadth of areas covered increases with each problem. It is best to start with Problem 1 and work through them in order, as some later problems will build on points made in earlier problems.

Each problem is firstly set out with suggested issues you might consider and references to more information on law and ethics within Dale and Appelbe's *Pharmacy Law and Ethics*. We think the best way to tackle them is to cover up everything except the problem to start with and see what issues you can identify. Then compare them with our list. You can then go on to write down your existing knowledge of the law and ethical rules applying to these issues before looking up the references given later on the page.

When you have done that, try to carry out a full analysis of the problem using the procedure outlined in the previous section. Then you can turn the page to see how we have worked through the procedure to come to our own conclusions. We think you might need about half an hour to 'crack' each problem, perhaps a little longer for those situations that are the least familiar to you.

Each problem has a fully worked solution. In addition, at the end of some of them, there are 'variations on the same theme' which you might like to tackle or bring to a group discussion. Have a go at thinking up your own variations and compare your reasoning with those of your colleagues. By practising and taking your time to solve these examples, you will find it much easier to respond to similar problems when they arise in real life.

PROBLEM ONE

Who decides what is an emergency?

In the past pharmacists had no discretion whatsoever over the supply of Prescription Only Medicines (POMs). Giving a salbutamol inhaler to an asthmatic or supplying two tablets of phenytoin to an epileptic who had come away on holiday without medication were criminal offences. In 1983, the 'emergency supply provisions' (under the Medicines Act) were introduced (Chapter 7), and these recognised that life throws up all sorts of situations where patients are in 'immediate need' of prescription medicines but do not have any with them.

The law, as always, lays down only minimum conditions for an 'emergency supply' and the Code of Ethics provides a principled context by saying that pharmacists must use their knowledge for the wellbeing and safety of patients and the public. But no rulebook can cover every situation that the practising pharmacist may have to face.

Try this problem:

The weekend visit of the mother who has diabetes

Mrs Fraser comes into your pharmacy on Saturday afternoon and says that her mother, who has diabetes and is frail, is at Mrs Fraser's home in quite a state. Her mother has come to stay for the weekend and forgot to pack her tablets. Mrs Fraser has tried ringing her own local surgery but could get no reply. What can you do to help?

<table>
<tr><td>What
issues
should I
consider?</td><td>

- criteria for making an 'emergency supply';
- restrictions on the supply of POMs;
- the principles of negligence;
- key responsibilities of a pharmacist in the Code of Ethics;
- limits of vicarious liability;
- therapeutics – management of diabetes;
- good practice – use of patient medication records.

</td></tr>
<tr><td>Where should
I look in
Pharmacy
Law & Ethics?</td><td>

- 'emergency supply' (Chapter 7);
- supplies of POMs (Chapter 7);
- negligence (Chapter 20);
- Code of Ethics (Chapter 20);
- vicarious liability (Chapter 25).

</td></tr>
</table>

Stage 1: gather relevant facts

Of course you will try to establish the name and other details of the medicine(s) being taken by Mrs Fraser's mother. Then move to decision-making.

What criminal law applies here?

Normally, POMs may only be supplied against the written authority of a medical practitioner. Before even contemplating an 'emergency supply at the request of a patient', there are a number of preconditions which can be summarised as follows.

The pharmacist must interview the person requesting the medicine and be satisfied that:

- there is an immediate need for the POM; and
- it is impracticable to obtain a prescription without undue delay; and
- the person requesting the medicine has had it prescribed for them before; and
- the details of the dose to be taken are established.

Note that there is no mention of 'emergency' or a definition of what that term means. The test is whether you, as the supplying pharmacist, are satisfied that there is an 'immediate need' and that it is impracticable to obtain a prescription. To assess this, you will want more information on both Mrs Fraser's mother's condition and treatment and the local arrangements for contacting a doctor. Moreover, the regulations assume the person who is requesting the medicine is the patient and can be personally interviewed so that you can establish what the medication is, its previous prescription and dose. In this case, the patient is not in the pharmacy.

What NHS law applies here?

Strictly speaking, none at all. The 'emergency supply' arrangements mean that you can sell or supply POMs without the authority of a prescription, subject to all the legal requirements. Most patients who are in need of continuous medication will be NHS patients and may be unwilling or unable to pay for medicines that they would otherwise obtain at no cost under the NHS. So can you ask for payment that is refundable when a subsequent NHS prescription is presented? Yes. The law does not address the question of payment; that is entirely up to you.

You may have to cope with repeated requests in advance of NHS prescriptions by patients who seem to run out of medication on a regular basis. Each one may well demonstrate an 'immediate need', but remember that the 'emergency supply' provisions are intended for isolated and unprecedented circumstances, not for the regular circumvention of local arrangements for obtaining repeat prescriptions and, in any event, you may only give a maximum of five days' supply in most cases.

What civil law applies here?

A useful way to answer this is to consider the consequences of supplying the medication and then the consequences of not supplying. If you do supply the medication, then you will assume liability for its being correctly identified, at the right strength and dose and for the advice and guidance you may give to Mrs Fraser as to what further action she might need to take. If you decide not to supply, then you might also be held liable for any adverse consequences to both mother and daughter. However, in both cases the likelihood of action against you (or even criticism of you) will depend upon what the 'reasonably competent pharmacist' would have done in these circumstances. This is an important principle followed in negligence cases (often called the 'Bolam test' after the name of the respondent in an important case) and one which is regularly used to judge whether action or inaction by a professional person was reasonable.

What guidance does the Code of Ethics give here?

Your key responsibility is to use your knowledge for the wellbeing and safety of Mrs Fraser's mother. Is this an emergency? If so, standard 15 of the Code picks up the civil law approach by saying you should consider the medical consequences of not supplying the medication.

What professional knowledge do I have which applies here?

You will already have drawn on your academic knowledge of diabetes and the medicines used to manage it. You might have briefly considered whether there were any substitute medicines that were not Prescription Only that may have been suitable for the condition, or whether dietary advice alone might be sufficient. You will need to know how long Mrs Fraser's mother is staying; if this is more than five days, the appropriate course might include making arrangements for a prescription to be obtained for further supplies. You will take into account the age of the patient and circumstances such as mobility and transport arrangements for the patient and add to this your knowledge of local surgery hours and availability of local doctors. These will all be factors in helping you decide whether there is an 'immediate need' for the medication and whether it is 'impracticable' to obtain an authorising prescription.

Where can I look or who can I ask for help?

The most accessible summary of emergency supply requirements in the pharmacy is in the annual *Medicines, Ethics & Practice* guide published by the RPSGB. Virtually all pharmacies have patient medication records, or you may be able to telephone the pharmacy used by Mrs Fraser's mother. Location of the patient's details could confirm exactly what has been prescribed and when. In other circumstances, the empty bottle of medication could substantiate its identity; sometimes the enquirer will have a repeat medication card with them or the 'repeat slip' from a computer-printed prescription.

Finally, you could try yourself to contact the doctor used by Mrs Fraser's mother and verify her treatment with the medical records or contact any out-of-hours GP service to see if the supply can be authorised by a prescription. In this last case, you will then have converted the situation into one of 'emergency supply at the request of a doctor' for which he or she undertakes to provide you with an authorising prescription within 72 hours.

Stage 2: prioritise and ascribe values

Patient

By this stage you will not have much difficulty in knowing that your prime objective is establishing whether it is in the interests of the patient to make the supply and deciding that it is.

Patient's relatives, carers and contacts

Mrs Fraser also wishes to avoid having to deal with the consequences of her mother not receiving the medication that she needs and, again, you are in a position to help.

Other healthcare professionals, your profession

Your duty as a pharmacist will mean that you should take reasonable steps to involve a medical practitioner in the care of Mrs Fraser's mother if at all possible. If this is not possible, then you may resort to your authority to use the 'emergency supply' provisions. Remember that you may also make 'emergency supplies' of POMs at the request of a doctor, and these supplies are not subject to quantity restrictions (Chapter 7).

Employer

The decision to provide an 'emergency supply' provision is very much a personal one, and one for which the individual pharmacist is accountable, so this scenario represents a good example of a situation in which you have the opportunity to exercise your own professional judgement. Your employer would therefore expect you to take the decision on that basis.

Self

This case is relatively straightforward in that diabetes is a condition that requires continuous medication control, and there is little of moral or cultural concern in deciding to make the supply. We discuss more difficult situations at the end of this exercise and in Problem 2.

Stage 3: generate options

What *could* you do?

1 Do not make the supply.
2 Do not make the supply and suggest further action.
3 Make the supply in accordance with the 'emergency supply' provisions.
4 Contact a doctor and make an emergency supply on his or her instructions.
5 Delay to seek advice.

You should then consider the likely outcome of each option.

If you followed option 1, Mrs Fraser's mother would be likely to become hyperglycaemic and possibly seriously ill. At the weekend, when accident and emergency services are likely to be at full stretch, it would be hard to defend this option as being the action of a responsible pharmacist. Option 2 might be defensible if you can locate a doctor who could readily supply a prescription, but that prescription would have to be dispensed somewhere (unless the doctor can make his own supply) so you would have to consider the local arrangements for weekend dispensing. The patient might have had other medication which could be used as a stopgap to control her condition, but we know that this is not so in this case. Option 4 is only possible if you can contact a doctor, but it can be useful for borderline cases of emergency supply on your own authority. Option 5 is unlikely to be helpful unless the advice you seek is immediately to hand.

Stage 4: choose an option

What *should* you do?

We think you should choose option 3 – do you agree?

We have identified 3 as the best option and the one that is defensible in the interests of the patient. We should ask, 'defensible to whom?'.

The patient is unlikely to object, and neither is her daughter, Mrs Fraser, but there is a snag – you have not interviewed the person for whom the medicine is intended and have therefore not fully complied with the law. The regulations refer only to the interview of the 'person requesting', but indicate later that this phrase is intended to mean the patient by saying that the medicine should have been prescribed previously for 'the person requesting the medicine'. One way of overcoming this aspect of the problem might be to ring Mrs Fraser's mother, i.e. conduct the interview over the telephone. You would need to be sure the person you were talking to was Mrs Fraser's mother. Alternatively, you could offer to deliver the medicine personally and conduct the interview with Mrs Fraser's mother at home.

Who else might challenge you? The RPSGB's inspector, your own staff, other pharmacists, the GP who looks after Mrs Fraser's mother? When making the supply you have to make a written record of the details, including a note on the 'nature of the emergency'. This is where you write your defence. Write down the circumstances that led to your decision – the time of day, the nature of the patient's condition, the questions you asked, the facts you established – all of these will justify your professional judgement that giving a limited quantity of the patient's oral antidiabetic tablets was the right thing to do.

Discussion points

We have seen how the 'test' for making an 'emergency supply' depends upon whether the pharmacist is satisfied that there is an immediate need for the medication and that it is impracticable in the circumstances to obtain a prescription. Although 'emergency supply' is frequently an issue for community pharmacists, exactly the same law and ethical requirements applies to requests made in the hospital setting. Consider whether you think the following circumstances meet the emergency supply criteria and apply the above analysis to your decisions as to what you would do.

- The same request is made on a bank holiday.
- The same request is made on a Saturday morning and your pharmacy is open until 6.00 p.m.
- The same request is made in your late-night pharmacy at 8.00 p.m. on Tuesday and there is a visitors' clinic at the local surgery every Wednesday afternoon.
- The same request is made over the telephone.
- The same request is made but the patient is visiting from Bangladesh.
- You are an on-call hospital pharmacist dealing with the same request at 10 p.m. on Saturday evening.
- The request is for epilepsy medication for a three-year-old who is at home with the baby sitter.
- The request is made when the local surgery is open but is for a salbutamol inhaler and the patient is in front of you showing the early signs of an asthma attack.

Rational decisions: palliative care versus drug abuse

We shall explore the 'emergency supply' situation a little further before going on to other matters. Let us consider the following two situations:

The clumsy toddler and the spilt medicines

You have been managing a pharmacy for several years when, on a Sunday rota, Mrs Baker comes in looking very agitated. You know that Mrs Baker's mother is being nursed at home after a diagnosis of terminal stomach cancer. Mrs Baker says that her toddler has knocked over and spilt all of the diamorphine solution prescribed for her mother and she has been unable to contact any doctor for assistance. What do you do?

You have been managing a pharmacy for several years when, on a Sunday rota, Ms Slade comes in looking very agitated. Ms Slade is a drug abuser to whom you have been supplying methadone mixture for nearly six months under the NHS arrangements for supplies by instalments to drug abusers. Ms Slade says her toddler has knocked over and spilt all of the methadone mixture you gave her yesterday and she has been unable to contact any doctor for assistance. What do you do?

What issues should I consider?	■ criteria for making an 'emergency supply';
	■ restrictions on supply of controlled drugs;
	■ the principles of negligence;
	■ key responsibilities of a pharmacist in the Code of Ethics;
	■ therapeutics – management of palliative care and drug abuse;
	■ local knowledge of support services.
Where should I look in Pharmacy Law & Ethics?	■ 'emergency supply' (Chapter 7);
	■ supplies of controlled drugs (Chapter 16);
	■ negligence (Chapter 20);
	■ Code of Ethics (Chapter 20).

Would you take the same action in both cases? If not, on what basis do you distinguish between the two sets of circumstances and how do you justify your position? Let's try some analysis.

Stage 1: gather relevant facts

What criminal law applies here?

It will be the same in both cases. The Misuse of Drugs Act 1971 makes no distinction between medical use and abuse of controlled drugs. Schedule 2 and 3 controlled drugs cannot be supplied under the 'emergency supply of POMs' exemptions; indeed, controlled drugs cannot be supplied to patients at all unless you have a valid written authorisation in your possession at the time of supply. You are also legally required to record in the controlled drug register every supply of a Schedule 2 controlled drug that you make.

What NHS law applies here?

None – but see Problem 1.

What civil law applies here? What guidance does the Code of Ethics give here?

As described in Problem 1, the same requirement to behave as would any 'reasonably competent' pharmacist applies to both these situations. One consequence of not supplying in Ms Slade's case might be that she could commit a crime or cause trouble if she is without her methadone.

What professional knowledge do I have which applies here?

You will have detailed knowledge of the action and uses of diamorphine from your undergraduate studies, together with an understanding of cancer and its effects. You will know that it is as valuable sometimes for its euphoric action as much as the relief of pain in terminal conditions. Are there any substitutes for diamorphine that you can legally supply? Perhaps a Prescription Only analgesic that has been prescribed before? Further questions might elicit what other medicines are available to Mrs Baker's mother and how well they may manage the degree of pain involved.

You should also understand something of addiction and the importance of maintenance treatment. You may also know that Ms Slade's prescription is sent to you by the local drug abuse clinic and she has a supply authorised for tomorrow, Monday.

Where can I look or who can I ask for help?

This is where you will have to be very enterprising. Mrs Baker's mother will suffer if she does not have her diamorphine. Where can you contact a medical practitioner? Perhaps there is a deputising doctors' co-operative available; a deputising doctor who understands your problem may well be willing to come to your pharmacy and write a prescription. This illustrates the importance of developing and maintaining good relationships with other healthcare professionals. You are much more likely to resolve these kind of problems if you know the doctor you are speaking to and have perhaps helped out with advice or information in the past.

Alternatively, could the local hospital find a doctor who would be prepared to authorise the supply? Are there any other pharmacists in the area who could suggest other doctors? If these are possibilities, can Mrs Baker get to these doctors and will there be a pharmacy open when she does? Could you possibly stay open until a prescription arrives or could you come back specially to dispense the prescription? Could you offer to deliver the medicine after the doctor agrees to call in and give you a prescription? Have you thought about the exemption that allows you to supply a controlled drug to a doctor on the personal promise of a written requisition within 24 hours?

Are you going to make the same effort for Ms Slade? If not, why not? Might there be further evidence you would require from Ms Slade?

Stage 2: prioritise and ascribe values

Patient

Mrs Baker's mother is being cared for at home and, as she has been prescribed diamorphine, is probably close to death. Lack of diamorphine for her may result in significant pain and distress and may even hasten death. Ms Slade is reasonably fit but will certainly suffer some discomfort and distress if she does not have her regular methadone. She might be tempted to use inappropriate substances to satisfy her cravings, which could potentially cause her death.

Patients' relatives, carers, grandchildren, contacts

Mrs Baker is already looking after her mother and a toddler. She will be distressed if her mother suffers; could this compromise the care of the toddler?

Is it possible that the toddler may have ingested any of the medicine in either case? Ms Slade also has a toddler in her charge and indicates that she will have to 'go out and score' if she does not have her methadone. She may therefore represent a risk to her child, colleagues, neighbours or the general public if she is without her methadone.

Other healthcare professionals, your profession

As in Problem 1, your duty is to involve a doctor if at all possible, and this is strengthened by the serious sanctions that may be used against you if you supply a controlled drug without authorisation. Set against this is an over-riding obligation to do what you can to help the patients.

Yourself

Your attitude to these two cases is likely to be different. You may well want to do anything you can to help Mrs Baker; you may be less willing for Ms Slade. Such differences may arise for many reasons. You may have had experience of nursing someone with cancer and empathise with Mrs Baker. You may have experienced or heard of colleagues' experiences with addicts, who not infrequently lie to obtain extra supplies of their medication. You may not feel too sympathetic to either situation when you have given up your precious Sunday to do a rota.

As a pharmacist, your decision to help must not be based on emotion or personal prejudice; you must be able to justify your action on rational grounds.

Stage 3: generate options

What *could* you do?

1 Do not supply.
2 Do not supply but suggest further action.
3 Do supply enough for immediate need.
4 Delay and seek further advice.

Let us consider the consequences of each option and introduce another concept: probability. We have seen that all sorts of things might happen as a result of the choice you make but, then again, they might not. What is the likelihood in each case?

We think that option 1 is not defensible in either case. There is a high probability of adverse effects for both patients if you do nothing. We would not recommend option 3 because of the criminal sanctions you would incur, although it might conceivably be an option in an extreme emergency. Option 4, which might at first sight seem unhelpful, could be very useful if the delay can be short. If you said, 'Can you call back in half an hour while I try to sort things out', this will allow you time to collect your thoughts, finish what you were in the middle of, delegate some tasks to others, make phone calls in the absence of the enquirer, who may be anxious or oppressive, and allow time for discussion with colleagues or check records.

Stage 4: choose an option

What *should* you do?

We think option 4 followed by option 2 is defensible. Do you agree?

Note that Problem 1 looked at a situation where a supply under the 'emergency supply' provisions was defensible, whereas Problem 2 looks at a situation where they cannot be used. It is the pharmacist who judges the 'immediate need' and the 'practicability' of obtaining a prescription. The pharmacist will also inevitably use his or her own judgement as to whether or not the patient's need is urgent. We also recommend that you keep the patient or customer informed about what is happening, explain to them the reasons for the decisions you take and make a record of your actions even if you decide not to supply.

Discussion points

Consider the following requests which arise on that Sunday rota, how you might respond and analyse your reasons.

- A request for sleeping tablets which have just run out.
- A request for tablets to manage depression which have just run out.
- A request for the 'after sex' pill (we go into this in more detail in Problem 15).

PROBLEM THREE

A real emergency

The previous two problems dealt with urgent situations which may or may not have been emergencies. When you look at the regulations for 'emergency supply' you will see that these words do not appear in the relevant regulations, apart from in the records you must make. Also, a careful study of the regulations suggests that the circumstances envisaged do not equate to the dictionary definition of an 'emergency', i.e. a state of danger, a life-threatening condition. Moreover, the fact that the regulations permit the supply of oral contraceptives and of original packs of ointments and creams reinforces the view that the legislators were not contemplating situations which were immediately life-threatening[1]. However, in our third problem we consider a real emergency.

The teenager and the coleslaw salad

You are the pharmacist in charge of a busy in-store pharmacy within a large edge-of town supermarket. You cover three 12-hour shifts on alternate days mid-week and it is nearing 2.00 p.m. when you take your lunch break. You hear a commotion outside the dispensary and find a small group of customers looking anxiously at a teenage girl who is sitting on the floor. She is very distressed, having difficulty in breathing and her face, especially her lips, are swollen. She manages to tell you that she has a peanut allergy and thinks there must have been some in the coleslaw salad she had just eaten in the supermarket café. Her friend hands you an Epipen that she's found in the casualty's handbag and asks you to administer it. What will you do?

What issues should I consider?	■ criteria for making an 'emergency supply'; ■ administration of parenteral POMs; ■ the principles of negligence and a duty of care; ■ key responsibilities of a pharmacist in the Code of Ethics; ■ the nature of anaphylactic shock and its treatment; ■ local knowledge of support services, in-store and elsewhere; ■ professional indemnity insurance or other cover.
Where should I look in Pharmacy Law & Ethics?	■ Criteria for making an 'emergency supply' (Chapter 7); ■ administration of parenteral POMs (Chapter 7); ■ the principles of negligence (Chapter 20); ■ key responsibilities of a pharmacist in the Code of Ethics (Chapter 20).

Stage 1: gather relevant facts

What criminal law applies here?

We set out the conditions for making an 'emergency supply' at this stage in Problem 1. We do not think you will have any difficulty in deciding that this is an emergency, although you would ordinarily have to establish whether the casualty had received the medication before. In the Medicines Act, no one is allowed to administer POMs unless to themselves or by or acting in accordance with the instructions of a 'practitioner'. There are a number of exemptions, however, for some parenteral injections for the purpose of saving a human life in an emergency. The list includes adrenaline injection.

What NHS law applies here?

None.

What civil law applies here?

The legal position on the obligation to render first aid is perhaps surprising. UK civil law has no 'Good Samaritan' expectations that citizens will go to the help of others when they are in danger. Thus, strictly speaking, you have no more obligation than, say, the café waitress or the till operators to help this teenager in distress. If you were, for example, a trained first-aider and had a badge or a notice saying that you were, then the expectation might be different. By advertising your special skill, you may be considered to have a 'duty of care' to render first-aid to those who seek such help.

The position of pharmacists or other healthcare professionals who are in contact with the public is less clear, since there is a widespread expectation from the public that all healthcare professionals will be able to help and, what's more, will do so. Here, the danger is of attempting to help beyond your competence. No claim in negligence could result from a failure to help; if you claimed to be competent to help and then performed less than competently, a claim in negligence could conceivably arise.

Set against this is well-established case law[2] that first-aiders are not expected to be miracle workers. In the classic situation where a passenger has a heart attack on an aeroplane and a fellow traveller who happens to be a heart surgeon offers to treat him, the surgeon is not expected to deliver the same standard of care as he would if he were working back home in his operating theatre.

What guidance does the Code of Ethics give here?

Rightly or wrongly, the public does look to pharmacists to render first-aid in many situations. The need to demonstrate an awareness of emergency first-aid features amongst the performance indicators expected in order to register as a pharmacist. The key responsibility of a pharmacist to use their knowledge for the wellbeing and safety of patients and the public must imply a responsibility to be prepared to give first-aid, if at all practicable. This expectation is reinforced by standard 15 of the Code of Ethics.

Where can I look or who can I ask for help?

Leaving aside for the moment that in reality you would have no time for consultation, what might you do to anticipate such problems in the future? What do you know about the treatment of anaphylactic shock? What does this condition look like? What presentations of parenteral adrenaline are available and how are they administered? How do patients use Epipen? Can it be administered through clothing? Are there any trained first-aiders amongst the supermarket staff? Are there any procedures already in place for dealing with such an emergency? You will know how to telephone the emergency services, but do you know how long it may take them to reach the supermarket? Are there any surgeries within immediate reach?

In the introduction, we talked about the concept of clinical governance and risk management. Did you know that there is a dummy version of Epipen available that you could practice with? Giving some thought to what might happen and making preparations to deal with problems before they happen is a major part of good clinical practice; it will also help you to sleep more easily at night!

Stage 2: prioritise and ascribe values

Patient

You will have no difficulty in deciding that your overriding priority is to do whatever you can to save the life of the teenager who has collapsed in your pharmacy.

Patient's friend, onlookers, your staff

The utility of others in this setting is to do something useful! Get someone to ring for an ambulance, find the first-aider, run to the surgery, read out the instructions on the Epipen.

Other healthcare professionals, your profession, your employer

Your ability to cope with crises such as this will reflect on the standing of pharmacists in general and of your employer with the outside world. Whilst not an immediate priority right now, you will want to bear this in mind in the future. You will also not want to be worrying about whether you are insured for your contemplated actions or whether your employer will cover you; check this out before you start your employment.

Yourself

Leaving aside the legalities and professional imperatives governing the action you will take, nothing will be as difficult to live with as the knowledge that you might have been able to save someone's life and did not try. This will bear heavily on your choice of action.

Stage 3: generate options

What *could* you do?

1   Do nothing.

As a conscious decision we think you will have little difficulty in recognising this is an option which would be difficult to defend. Worse, you may be perceived as callously doing nothing, simply because you don't know what to do.

2   Call for medical assistance.

This is certainly the least you can do, is it not? Call for the emergency services and call for internal support as well. Don't overlook a check on whether the friend or even the bystanders have any knowledge about using Epipen.

3　　Administer the Epipen yourself.

The merit of this option will depend very much on the outcome. You could save a life or watch it being lost despite your efforts. Even very prompt administration of adrenaline is not always successful; inept administration, especially by the wrong route, might just make things worse. Do you have another option?

4　　Help the friend to administer the Epipen.

Is this any better than option 3? Both will depend on how much knowledge is possessed by the person doing the administration. When individuals are aware that they have a severe allergy and are prescribed medicines like Epipen, they should be given clear instructions on how to use them. Perhaps the casualty has shared this knowledge with her friend?

Stage 4: choose an option

What *should* you do?

We think that unless you could be very sure that the friend knew what to do, we would choose option 3. Do you agree? There is little tradition in this country of being sued for failed emergency first-aid, although it is possible. We think it is much more likely that there would be criticism and even adverse publicity if you did not try to help, however inexpertly.

Discussion

We hope very much that you are never challenged by a scenario such as this, although it is drawn from real life. Clearly the counsel of perfection is to find out how to deal with such eventualities before they happen. We give a few more examples of preparing for risks in later problems. You might also like to consider the legal and ethical aspects of the following variation.

■　　The same request arises where the patient is a child on the verge of an asthma attack and his mother is so panic-stricken that she hands you his inhaler to administer.

References

1 Harrison I. 'What constitutes an emergency?' *Pharm J* 18 June 1988 p.783.
2 Bateman R. V. (1925) 94 LJKB 791 at 794, CCA.

PROBLEM FOUR

Recycling medicines
for the Third World

As a pharmacist, you are responsible for safeguarding the quality of the medicines you supply and for using your knowledge to ensure that no one is put at risk from defective medicines. Establishing the origin and history, i.e. the provenance, of medicines is part of your duty as a pharmacist. Try to deal with this problem.

> **The priest in Ethiopia**
>
> You receive a phone call from Mr Jarvis, whom you know to be a local priest who has just returned from working in Ethiopia. He wants to return there every few months to help in the medical outposts in the rural areas and is very anxious to take with him any medicines you can spare. He wants to collect any medicines you have that have been returned by patients. Can you help?

What issues should I consider?

- restrictions on supply of POMs;
- rules on wholesale dealing;
- rules on environmental protection and waste disposal;
- the principles of negligence;
- key responsibilities of a pharmacist in the Code of Ethics;
- law and ethics facts sheets on this subject, which include World Health Organization guidelines;
- knowledge of pharmaceutics, especially stability and potency;

- good professional practice;
- use of outside resources, for example, employer, professional organisations.

Where should
I look in
Pharmacy
Law & Ethics?

- supplies of POMs (Chapter 7);
- wholesale dealing (Chapter 9);
- environmental protection (Chapter 25);
- negligence (Chapter 20);
- Code of Ethics (Chapter 20).

Stage 1: gather relevant facts

What criminal law applies here?

When medicines are issued to patients they are then the property of those patients. If, however, they are voluntarily returned to you for disposal they become your property and change their status. Under environment protection legislation, POMs, which include controlled drugs, will also become 'special waste'. Certain medicines, such as cytotoxics, will also be classed as 'hazardous waste'. They have to be disposed of without risk to people or the environment and controlled drugs have to be 'denatured' so that they cannot be recovered and re-used. In the meantime you must store the returned medicines safely.

Making a supply of a POM for onward supply to someone else is a wholesale supply. Certain conditions must be met and records must be kept. A series of fact sheets are available from the Royal Pharmaceutical Society. The fact sheet on export of medicines includes guidance on drug donations to developing countries; a copy of the World Health Organization guidelines is also available from the Society.

What NHS law applies here?

The Terms of Service do not cover arrangements for taking back patients' medicines. Your local NHS health body should provide facilities at no charge so that a licensed waste disposal contractor takes away medicines which have been returned by patients.

What civil law applies here?

We have already discussed in the Introduction the fact that pharmacists have a 'duty to care' about all who seek to use their services; this would apply as much to potential patients in Ethiopia as to those in the UK. You should consider what steps you could take to ensure that the medicines you supply are what they say they are and that they are in good condition and fit for use. This could be a tall order when applied to returned medicines. How do you know what has happened to them while in the patient's possession?

What guidance does the Code of Ethics give here?

Your key responsibility is to use your knowledge for the wellbeing and safety of patients and the public. Standard 2 in the Code, which relates to stock, says that medicines returned to a pharmacy from a patient's home, a nursing or residential home must not be supplied to any other patient. This standard also spells out your duty of care to exercise control over 'any medicine, food supplement or healthcare related product' by saying that you must not supply if you have reason to doubt its quality or safety. You should also note a clause in standard 4, which allows the reissue of patient's own medicines in the hospital context, under certain conditions.

So you might think that this means that you cannot help Mr Jarvis; not so. The law and ethics fact sheet mentioned above sets out a series of conditions, derived from World Health Organization guidelines, under which you might be able to help after all.

Finally, standard 4 on pharmacy premises and facilities, and standard 16 on collection and disposal of pharmaceutical waste make it clear that, in accepting back such medicines, you would be expected to have in place instructions on how to manage their temporary storage safely to minimise risk to patients, the public and staff.

What professional knowledge do I have which applies here?

This is an area where your pharmaceutical training should help. There will be some instances, perhaps when sealed original packs are returned, when the contents will be known with reasonable certainty. If the expiry date is some way distant, then they are more likely to be in good condition. If they have been stored in the medicines cabinet of a well-run nursing home, they are unlikely to have been subject to adverse storage conditions or to have been tampered with and so on. Only you, as the pharmacist, can assess these factors and then you will assume responsibility for deciding whether the medicines are fit for re-use. A good test might be whether you would be prepared to take them yourself!

There are other considerations. What kind of medicines do they want in Ethiopia? Almost certainly not antidepressants, hormone replacement therapy, anorexics or hypolipidaemic agents. They are much more likely to need anti-infectives, vaccines and analgesics. What kind of medicines do your patients return?

Where can I look or who can I ask for help?

If you are an employee, you employer might have a policy on such matters or might already be involved in existing schemes to help provide medicines to

Third World countries. Some Rotary clubs and similar organisations have local arrangements for collecting and sorting supplies for wider international schemes.

Stage 2: prioritise and ascribe values

Patients, relatives, carers, contacts

Significant quantities of drug donations made in response to local disasters in the Third World have been reported to be useless or, worse, have tied up resources in sorting and disposing of them which could have been better used (see Discussion). People in the Third World have an equal right to those in the First World to receive medicines that are fit to use and appropriate for their needs. Those trying to help them do not want to waste their time sorting out the identity of medicines and trying to guess whether they are of value. So your duty as a pharmacist is to provide only that which it is in the patient's interest to receive. The World Health Organization guidance makes it clear that the recipients of any donations should provide a list of what is required.

Other healthcare professionals, your profession

In this case, Mr Jarvis does not indicate that he is working with any organised scheme that may include doctors and pharmacists in the assessment and sorting process. You should check whether this is the case; there may well be other schemes which focus on the needs of Ethiopia, to which Mr Jarvis can add his efforts.

Your employer

Because your employer would carry vicarious liability (Chapter 25) for what you do in this case, you must consult your employer if you have one. Activity in this area can be misconstrued by the media – think of headlines such as 'major company dumps inferior drugs on Third World' – and, as ever, you must be able to defend any decisions you have taken on which medicines to supply.

Yourself

Do you think it is right to supply medicines in the way Mr Jarvis suggests? You might feel it is more appropriate to provide money, either directly or through a national charity, to allow the purchase of 'new' medicines for

Ethiopia's needs. Or you might feel that you should help in whatever way you can as such medicines will otherwise simply be destroyed. You might even have preferences for which countries should be helped, but this should not be allowed to obscure your objective professional judgement on what you should do. Finally, we have given you an example in which you know something about the enquirer, Mr Jarvis. As a pharmacist, you also have a duty not to be gullible – can you think of other situations when you might be wise to consider exactly what the recipient might do with any returned medicines you supplied?

Stage 3: generate options

What *could* you do?

Let us suggest the following:

1   Say you cannot help Mr Jarvis.
2   Agree to supply returned medicines to Mr Jarvis if he would like to come and collect them.
3   Make supply direct to the mission hospital on Mr Jarvis's instructions.
4   Delay and seek advice.
5   Ask Mr Jarvis for a written proposal as to what he wants to do.
6   Ask Mr Jarvis to come to your pharmacy and discuss his proposal with you.
7   Donate non-medicinal items instead, such as plasters, bandages and dressings.

A detailed analysis of the consequences of these options is probably unnecessary. Option 1 is 'safe', but more would be expected of the reasonably competent pharmacist. Option 2 is definitely 'unsafe' for the reasons already discussed. Option 3 would be lawful but would still be 'unsafe' without a great deal more enquiry. Option 4 will give you an opportunity to make a considered decision. Do not allow yourself to be rushed unnecessarily by pressure such as suggestions that other local pharmacies have supplied Mr Jarvis without any reluctance. If you seek advice from your employer you may find that they already participate in national schemes and would not wish to donate locally.

Options 5, 6 and 7 are all reasonable, depending on what further information you can elicit.

Stage 4: choose an option

What *should* you do?

We think option 4 is the best choice, followed perhaps in due course by 5, 6, 7, or even 1, if appropriate. Do you agree?

Discussion

New guidelines from the World Health Organization, published in 1996 (*Pharm J* 18 May 1996 p.672), emphasised that drug donations to needy areas must not be made without close communication between donors and recipients about real needs.

You might like to look up the case of a pharmacist who was 'struck off' after, among other things, misappropriating drugs donated by a pharmaceutical manufacturer on the understanding that they would be sent for relief of a disaster in Poland (*Pharm J* 29 July 1996 p.91).

PROBLEM FIVE

Protecting the reputation
of the profession

We have seen in Problem 4 that the pharmacist is rightly regarded as the custodian of the nation's drugs and the expert when it comes to establishing the provenance of medicines. Sometimes you will discover situations where your loyalties are exposed to scrutiny. Consider this case.

The residential home and the 'rogue' tablets

You are a community pharmacist and have just signed a contract to provide a pharmaceutical service to several residential homes. On your first visit to one of them, The Willows, you find in the medicines cupboard a large plastic pot with the remnants of a Brufen label on it. The pot now contains about a hundred unmarked pink tablets. A label from another pharmacy has been added saying 'painkillers'. What would you do?

What issues should I consider?
- nature and quality of the medicine;
- Medicines Act labelling regulations;
- possibility of fraud, 'passing off';
- NHS Terms of Service – 'as so ordered';
- the principles of negligence;
- key responsibilities of a pharmacist in the Code of Ethics;
- standard 2 on stock;

- therapeutics – use of non-steroidal anti-inflammatory drugs;
- local knowledge of other healthcare professionals;
- use of outside resources, e.g. employer, professional organisation.

Where should I look in Pharmacy Law & Ethics?

- nature and quality of medicines (Chapter 13);
- labelling regulations (Chapter 14)
- NHS Terms of Service (Chapter 23)
- negligence (Chapter 20)
- Code of Ethics (Chapter 20).

Stage 1: gather relevant facts

What criminal law applies here?

There are a number of possibilities. The staff at the residential home may have changed the tablets or the container themselves. The supplying pharmacist may simply have provided an additional label for them to use. This is not an offence, although it will probably breach the conditions for the home to be registered with the local authority and indicates poor practice on the part of the supplying pharmacist. Remember that Brufen tablets are a POM and may not be supplied within the NHS 'bulk prescribing' arrangements, nor would they be classed as 'homely remedies' that the home staff might acquire for themselves.

Remember, too, that in residential homes, clients are cared for as they would be in their own home. It is possible that a resident has chosen to take his or her own prescription to a specific pharmacy or has made a special request that the medicines should be dispensed by a specific pharmacy. Residents may go home for the weekend or go on holiday and obtain emergency prescriptions, etc. Thus, there may be several different pharmacies supplying medication for patients in residential homes.

It is also possible that the pharmacy supplying most of the medication for the residents has provided a pot containing something other than Brufen, although it is to be hoped that it is ibuprofen in some form. Perhaps there was a shortage of Brufen and an equivalent was supplied instead. In this case, the supply has breached the Medicines Act labelling requirements, which is a criminal offence.

Worse, perhaps there was a deliberate attempt to 'pass off' the pink tablets as Brufen when they clearly are not. This, too, would be a breach of the Medicines Act and would also constitute fraud, both criminal offences. You would certainly consider whether this was because the product was illegally obtained, either through a perversion of the parallel import arrangements or by failing to go through the UK licensing arrangements at all (Chapter 2).

What NHS law applies here?

Most medication for residential homes is supplied against NHS FP10 or GP10 (in Scotland) prescriptions, although some homes may be for residents who are private patients. If the authorising NHS prescription specified Brufen and this was not supplied, the supplying pharmacy would be in breach of its NHS Terms of Service, which require the contractor to supply what the doctor ordered (Chapter 23).

In theory, at least, a doctor who is looking after residents on a private basis can acquire any medicines against a signed order and leave them at the home with instructions to the carers on when and to whom they should be administered. It is not unknown for NHS prescribers to supply a 'stock' of medicines and then write retrospective NHS prescriptions to cover supplies already made from stock. Such arrangements are a breach of the doctor's Terms of Service and, if known to the supplying pharmacist, could also place him or her at risk.

What civil law applies here?

Fraudulent supplies would be an obvious breach of the pharmacist's duty of care towards all patients who are the recipients of his or her services. If those patients suffered injury or adverse effects, perhaps in this case a diminution of analgesia or unexpected side-effects through taking a medicine that was not what it seemed, the supplying pharmacist would be liable for these consequences. The home staff, too, would expect medicines to be what they said they were and could use this situation to terminate their arrangements with the supplying pharmacy.

What guidance does the Code of Ethics give here?

Part of the key responsibilities of a pharmacist says you should not engage in any activity that may bring the profession into disrepute. It would be important not to jump to conclusions here – there might be a legitimate explanation, but there probably is not. How should you deal with the knowledge that a fellow pharmacist might not be behaving as he or she should?

This key responsibility and the associated standard on stock (standard 2) will apply here; pharmacists must ensure that there is certainty in establishing identity, origin and chain of supply for any medicine. The standard also says that medicines should stay within their original foil or blister packaging up to the time of dispensing. Why are there no markings on these pink tablets? Could they have been removed from their packaging to disguise their origin?

You might like to turn to Chapter 21 at this point, particularly the cases under Parallel Imports, which outline some unfortunate cases of pharmacists who markedly failed in their duty to protect the public from the risks associated with medicines of uncertain origin and quality.

Let us go even further and consider whether these medicines might be counterfeit. Again, standard 2 of the Code of Ethics gives further guidance – should you need it – saying that such material must be isolated from other medicines and that a pharmacist must report to the RPSGB or other appropriate body any discovery of suspected counterfeit medicines.

Finally there is a specific standard, standard 17, on advisory services to nursing and residential homes. It is not clear in this situation whether The Willows is contracted to receive an advisory service and you might want to find this out.

What professional knowledge do I have which applies here?

You will know what conditions Brufen is used for and what the effect might be if patients who needed Brufen did not receive it. You might ascertain the seriousness of the situation by asking care staff and patients how helpful the 'Brufen' was in controlling pain. In order to be registered the home will have to meet certain conditions, which will cover arrangements for the supply of medicines. For residential homes, this is likely to be the local social services authority. You could find out who carries out this task in your area.

Where can I look or who can I ask for help?

You will certainly make discreet inquiries of the care staff about this pot of 'Brufen' to ascertain whether any of your suspicions might be correct. You might be able to obtain further facts by asking about 'stock' supplies; perhaps this pot was the subject of a signed order from a doctor who looks after some patients in the home. Are there additional bottles marked 'Brufen' for individual patients and do these also contain unmarked pink tablets?

You may feel that this is going beyond your remit as a community pharmacist. Who else can you turn to? When talking to the care staff, they may have identified the local community services pharmacist, who often gives advice on the handling of medication in both nursing and residential homes. You might seek advice from this pharmacist; he or she might also know who carries out inspections in the Willows.

You will have reasonable misgivings about the legitimacy of this 'Brufen' and can seek advice from the RPSGB's local inspector. He or she could make many more enquiries than you and establish whether your concerns are justified. You might prefer to seek advice from your employers or the NPA and let them help you decide what the next steps should be.

Stage 2: prioritise and ascribe values

Patients, relatives, carers, contacts

You cannot tell for certain whether patients are at risk in this situation, but they certainly might be. You have a duty to take whatever action is necessary in the interests of the patient. At this stage this may mean no more than suggesting this 'Brufen' is left on one side for you to make enquiries, while making arrangements for a replacement supply. You might want to consider at what stage carers, relatives and others might expect to be aware of the situation; probably not until the facts have been more fully established.

Other healthcare professionals

In keeping with this approach, the patient's doctor might expect to know about this situation as soon as possible. Regrettably there have been cases of collusion between doctors and pharmacists to make fraudulent supplies of medicines, which suggests caution in informing the doctor just yet.[1,2,3] But if the pot of 'Brufen' is the doctor's stock and the care staff have been authorised to use it in prescribed circumstances, you might want to discuss alternative arrangements with the doctor or ask to see a clearly written account of what those 'prescribed circumstances' are.

Your profession

You are charged with behaving with 'dignity and probity' and you have discovered circumstances that may indicate that a pharmacist colleague has not been behaving professionally. Are you going to overlook this or report it? You also have a key responsibility to work in partnership with other health professions to provide the best possible healthcare for patients. Amongst the personal responsibilities of a pharmacist providing professional services is a requirement to report to the Society any concerns that a pharmacist's behaviour may be putting the public at risk. There is a clear likelihood that patients may suffer adverse consequences if medicines are not what they purport to be; co-operation is never intended to put patients at risk.

Yourself

Similar arguments may be applied to your own personal approach to such a situation. Do you think it is right to report a fellow pharmacist? Under what circumstances? Is there any other course of action that might be less contentious?

Stage 3: generate options

What *could* you do?

1   Do nothing.
2   Remove the pot of 'Brufen' and do nothing.
3   Remove or quarantine the pot of 'Brufen' and tell the care staff not to use it until you have made some enquiries.

Let us just stop here and consider consequences. If you select option 1, the patients may continue to be given tablets of unknown provenance. Moreover, if you select options 1 or 2, the pharmacist who made the original supply may continue to make similar supplies to patients in other homes or from the pharmacy, with possible risks to them all, particularly if they are elderly or confused.

Stage 4: choose an option

What *should* you do?

We think you'll have to take option 3. Do you agree?

Alas, you have not quite finished yet. What enquiries are you going to make? In a case like this, all you have is a number of facts and a few theories as to how these facts came about. Much more investigation is needed to draw any conclusions, and here help is at hand. We will go further and say we think you should pass this information to the RPSGB's inspector. Telephone the professionals standards department, outline your concerns and ask an inspector to call. Then it becomes their problem, not yours!

References

1   *Pharm J* 28 October 1995 p.573.
2   *Pharm J* 4 November 1995 p.606.
3   *Pharm J* 1 June 1996 p.745.

P R O B L E M   S I X

Responsibility for the supply of unlicensed medicines

You can rely on the existence of a marketing authorisation to guarantee the quality, safety and efficacy of most of the medicines that you supply. The holder of the marketing authorisation will also be liable for any adverse effects resulting from the use of his or her product. If you make up a medicine yourself in the pharmacy, say for a particular patient, you become liable for those aspects. What if a doctor prescribes a medicine for use in a way which is outside the marketing authorisation? Try this problem.

The child and the Phenergan Elixir

You are asked to check an NHS prescription calling for Phenergan Elixir for an 18-month-old child. Your dispenser tells you that, as the 'book' says that Phenergan should not be used in children aged under two, the surgery has been contacted and they have said it is OK to dispense. What would you do?

What issues should I consider?

- more facts – which 'book', who was spoken to and by whom?;
- medicines licensing requirements;
- exemptions for licensing for pharmacists;
- NHS Terms of Service – 'as so ordered';

- NHS 'blacklist';
- principles of negligence, liability for adverse effects, joint liability;
- key responsibilities of a pharmacist in the Code of Ethics;
- personal responsibilities of a pharmacist providing professional services;
- therapeutics – action and uses of promethazine;
- use of outside resource – drug information services;
- good practice – maintenance of records.

Where should I look in Pharmacy Law & Ethics?

- licensing of medicines (Chapter 2);
- exemptions from licensing for pharmacists (Chapter 2);
- NHS Terms of Service (Chapter 23);
- principles of negligence (Chapter 20);
- Code of Ethics (Chapter 20);
- joint liability (Chapter 20).

Stage 1: gather relevant facts

What criminal law applies here?

The legal category of a medicine is determined by its marketing authorisation and by legislation under the Medicines Act. Where a medicine is used in circumstances outside the marketing authorisation, supply may be unlawful unless there is an authorisation by a doctor to use it in this way. (Provided that the medicine does not appear on the POM list, there are circumstances when you may supply unlicensed medicines on your own authority; see 'counter prescribing' exemptions for pharmacists, Chapter 2.) In this case you have a valid prescription authorising supply.

What NHS law applies here?

The NHS Terms of Service require you to dispense 'drugs or medicines' as ordered by the doctor and that such supplies shall comply with appropriate standards such as the Drug Tariff, Ph. Eur., BPC and so forth (see Chapter 15). The Drug Tariff permits you to supply any medicine (i.e. not on the 'black list'; see Chapter 23), although the local health body can ask the prescriber to justify the prescription at a later stage. In practice, this rarely happens, and is particularly unlikely in this case as Phenergan is a licensed medicine and raises no issue for the Prescription Pricing Authority.

The Terms of Service also say that you must supply medicines with 'reasonable promptness' and do not allow for the possibility that the contractor may not wish, or refuse, to supply.

What civil law applies here?

All healthcare professionals have a 'duty to care' for the interests of the patients they serve. Thus, in prescribing a medicine for circumstances outside the marketing authorisation, the doctor has automatically assumed liability for any adverse effects that may result; conversely, the marketing authorisation holder (who is usually the manufacturer) would be entitled to disclaim all such liability.

What about you? As a pharmacist you also have a 'duty to care' about the patient. You may share liability with the doctor for any adverse effects resulting from a medicine that you supplied which you knew was going to be used outside the terms of its marketing authorisation. Precisely how much liability will depend upon how far you went ('reasonable steps') to establish that the doctor knew exactly what he or she was doing and what the consequences might be, and then took appropriate action to protect the patient's interests as well.

You might like to look now at two cases where joint liability, shared between doctor and pharmacist, resulted in substantial compensation (damages) being paid to the complainant (see negligence cases in Chapter 20).

What guidance does the Code of Ethics give here?

The Code of Ethics makes no specific reference to unlicensed medicines. However, extrapolating from your key responsibility to use your knowledge for the wellbeing and safety of patients and the public, you know that licensed medicines are of proven safety, quality and efficacy. So you could not use your exemption as a pharmacist to counter-prescribe unlicensed non-prescription medicines for whatever you fancied to recommend!

In addition, implicit in the key responsibilities is your duty to take whatever action is necessary in the interests of the patient, which will include a consideration of the consequences of supplying, or not supplying, the Phenergan Elixir. Moreover, the key responsibilities imply that you have a duty not to impair confidence in your own and other healthcare professions and to co-operate with colleagues to ensure patient benefit.

Support for these considerations is found in standard 4 on the supply of prescribed medicines, which says a licensed medicine should always be supplied, if available, in preference to an unlicensed one. The standard goes on to say that you should not substitute any other product for what is prescribed, except in an emergency or with consent, but your key responsibility for the safety of the patient may mean that in these circumstances, the right thing to do might be to refuse to dispense the prescription. This is an important example of a situation in which, although you have obligations under NHS law to dispense the prescription, your duty to the patient might override them.

What professional knowledge do I have which applies here?

You will already know, and can check in reference books, much about the various uses of promethazine. You will want more information about which of these uses is in the mind of the doctor on this occasion and what other medicines might be in use for this or other conditions. You might want to know whether the child has had Phenergan Elixir before and whether it was well tolerated. Your position might depend upon whether the treatment was initiated by a paediatrician for a specific symptom, for example, severe eczema which may be causing serious skin lesions through scratching, or prescribed more generally by the GP, for example, for itching associated with chicken pox. GPs prescribe Phenergan as a sedative for a fractious child, although this is not recommended if the child is below two years of age.

Where can I look or who can I ask for help?

The obvious source of information is the prescribing doctor, but you cannot be satisfied from the details you already have that he or she has been properly advised of the position. Who was spoken to at the surgery? Were the consequences of prescribing an unlicensed medicine properly explained? Has the person responsible for the patient been informed? *The Medicines Compendium, Martindale: The complete drug reference*, the BNF and a number of paediatric formularies prepared by specialist children's hospitals may give guidance on what doses may be suitable for a young child. Your local medicines information service or pharmacists and others at the local hospital pharmacy department may have experience of the use of promethazine in young children; your employer or the NPA may offer some guidance.

Stage 2: prioritise and ascribe values

Patient, parents, carers

You will need to establish exactly who is presenting the prescription for dispensing and what relationship they have to the child. If he or she knows what condition the Phenergan Elixir has been prescribed for, you could use this information to judge the consequences of supplying or not supplying. You should consider the consequences too for the child's carer. You have a duty to ensure that the carer understands that this is an unlicensed use of Phenergan Elixir (which will be difficult to explain in layman's terms), but you must achieve this without undermining their faith in either the medicine or the prescriber. The more information you have on the circumstances of its use, the easier it will be.

Other healthcare professionals, your profession

This is the tricky bit, especially as your dispenser has already contacted the surgery once. The marketing authorisation for Phenergan Elixir used to permit prescribing by doctors for children from one year of age, although supply over the counter was restricted to those aged two and over. If you ask your experienced colleagues, they will probably tell you that Phenergan Elixir was often prescribed for infants, indeed was often bought over the counter, for sedation – to 'give the parents a good night's sleep'. But are there other ways in which this could be achieved?

Before approaching any prescriber with the prospect of passing comment on his or her prescribing, you should be confident of being able to make constructive suggestions for alternatives that achieve the prescriber's intentions. Perhaps you could supply an alternative brand that is licensed for younger children (if you stock it). Or perhaps you could discuss what side-effects to be aware of and what advice the prescriber gave to the patient's carer or how he or she would like the position to be explained to them now.

Your employer

As with emergency supplies, the solution to this kind of problem very much depends on your personal judgement and accountability as a pharmacist. Although there may be many other pharmacists that you can call on for advice, what you actually do and how you do it will be largely up to you.

Yourself

We have already said that your duty as a pharmacist is to maintain confidence in your profession, and yourself as a member of it, and confidence in other healthcare professionals while at the same time ensuring that no patient is put at risk by, or at the very least is unaware of, the risks associated with using a medicine outside its marketing authorisation specifications. Your skill as a competent pharmacist is to carry out this task without alarming the patient (or in this case the parent or carer) or antagonising the prescriber.

Stage 3: generate options

What *could* you do?

1　Dispense the prescription with no further query or comment.
2　Check again with the surgery.

We think you will have little difficulty in recognising that you cannot just overlook this situation, so option 1 is not acceptable. Just take a little time to think about how the enquiries in option 2 should be made. You may get an indication of how urgent the prescription is by comparing the date on the prescription and the date it has been presented for dispensing. Should it be you or one of the staff who makes the enquiries? Will you settle for speaking to the receptionist or will you insist on the prescriber? What if he or she is not there? Will another doctor do? You will need the information about who has brought in the prescription as well. Is she the child's mother or a neighbour? If the latter, how will you ensure that the information is properly conveyed to the person who needs to know?

We think there are useful lessons here in planning how you are going to make your enquiries. Write down what information you need and tick it off when you get it. You'll want to avoid antagonising the doctor by asking the same questions about the same patients every month; could you check your patient medication record to see if any other pharmacist has recorded the response to similar enquiries. What adverse effects would you expect to see if promethazine were given to such a young child? Work out how you are going to ask the question – perhaps something like 'I haven't seen promethazine used in a child of this age before, could you please just confirm the background or rationale for choosing this particular drug and dose?'

So now you can generate some further options, provided you have ascertained what condition or symptoms are intended to be controlled and what alternatives (if any) you can suggest.

3   Attempt to persuade the prescriber to change the medication or agree to a modification in dose.

What if you cannot? You may need to demonstrate at some future stage that this phone call took place, so make a note of it in a permanent place and tell your colleagues that you have done so. In some situations you might even ask the prescriber to confirm in writing that he or she wants you to go ahead despite your advice. So there are more options:

4   Dispense the medication but explain to someone responsible for the patient about the situation and its consequences.
5   Refuse to dispense the medication but explain why to someone responsible for the patient.

Now let us consider the consequences of these last two options. The consequences of option 4 are unlikely, in this particular case, to be very serious. Phenergan Elixir has been used in very young children; you might consider supplying it and explaining to the child's parent or carer what you have done and why. Option 5 might be considered an over-reaction taking account of the Code of Ethics stricture to bear in mind the relative harm (and not just to the patient) that may result from such a refusal.

Stage 4: choose an option

What *should* you do?

We warned you in the introductory section on professional decision making that sometimes several options may have little attraction but that you might have to consider which, of a number of unsatisfactory solutions, did the least harm. On this basis therefore, we would choose option 4 – do you agree?

Discussion

Your choice of action could be entirely different if the facts were changed slightly. Consider the following situations, decide what you would do and why.

- The Phenergan Elixir is for a six-month-old infant.
- The Phenergan Elixir is for an 18-month-old child to control vomiting associated with chemotherapy.
- A customer comes to buy Phenergan Elixir for her 10-month-old child because the doctor has recommended she buy some to help her cope after the birth of her second child.

PROBLEM SEVEN

Responsibility for the supply of unlicensed medicines (2)

So far, we have looked at problems set in the community pharmacy practice sector. But the same laws and ethics apply just as well to hospital pharmacy practice. Pharmacy practice in hospitals must comply with the Medicines Act 1968 and the Misuse of Drugs Act 1971 and, of course, all pharmacists, wherever they work, are expected to comply with the profession's Code of Ethics. What is very different, however, is the application of internal NHS administrative directions, such as Health Service Circulars and guidance that constantly tell hospitals and other NHS bodies how they should carry out their work. Since the Health Act 1999 introduced a duty of quality for all NHS bodies, a whole performance assessment framework supported by controls assurance documents sets out in detail the quality objectives which should be reached within hospitals, with detailed audit and monitoring processes to ensure they are met. Whilst these instructions do not always strictly have legal force, many do and in a managed service the expectation is that they will be followed and in some instances, such as the requirements for Patient Group Directions, they are in excess of what is strictly required in law.

We will now look at a similar problem to Problem 6, but in a hospital setting.

> ### The midnight telephone call from the neonatal ward
>
> You are a recently qualified pharmacist and were appointed two weeks ago to a resident pharmacist post in a teaching hospital. At about midnight one night you get a call from a nurse on the neonatal unit requesting an unlicensed drug for administration to a neonate. You have never encountered this drug before. What do you do?

What issues should I consider?

- more facts – how urgently needed is this supply? Who is the original prescriber and can he or she be contacted? What reference source did the prescriber use? Is this a new prescription or a repeat order?;
- medicines licensing requirements;
- exemptions from licensing requirements for pharmacists;
- the law and Patient Group Directions;
- principles of negligence, joint liability;
- key responsibilities of a pharmacist in the Code of Ethics;
- ethical standards on Patient Group Directions;
- hospital policy in this situation;
- availability of alternative licensed medicines;
- hospital service policy on Patient Group Directions.

Where should I look in Pharmacy Law & Ethics?

- licensing of medicines (Chapter 2);
- exemptions from licensing for pharmacists (Chapter 2);
- Patient Group Directions (Chapters 7 and 8);
- principles of negligence, joint liability (Chapter 20);
- Code of Ethics (Chapter 20);
- hospital service directions (Chapter 27).

Stage 1: gather relevant facts

What criminal law applies here?

This will be exactly as set out in Problem 6. You should also consider the possibility that the nurse may be making this request within an authorising Patient Group Direction. These may be used to authorise the supply of medicines 'off-label' in certain circumstances, although this should be the exception rather than the rule. 'Off-label' is used to mean that the medicine has a marketing authorisation but the proposed conditions of use do not fall within the licensing conditions. A Patient Group Direction may not be used to authorise the supply of a medicine that has no licence at all.

What NHS law, including hospital service directions, applies here?

There are no explicit NHS legal provisions to cover this situation, although there is a Health Service Circular (in England) or equivalent setting out some additional conditions for Patient Group Directions. There should also be, within the hospital, policies and probably formularies on prescribing in neonatal or other practice or therapeutic areas in which the use of unlicensed medicines is commonplace.[1] As an on-call resident pharmacist you would be expected to be familiar with these. You should also be aware of any Patient Group Directions for 'off-label' use in operation in the hospital.[1]

What civil law applies here?

Again, your responsibilities and duty of care would be as in Problem 6. There is a further consideration that will have increasing impact on the quality expectations of pharmacy practice. The care and management of the neonate is generally recognised as a 'specialised' area, in which special expertise, over and above the 'reasonably competent' practitioner might be expected. In deciding whether your duty of care had been met, a court might also ask whether there was a recognised specialist body that sought to bring together specialised skills and knowledge in this area of practice. Although at the time of writing there was no such body, the College of Pharmacy Practice is establishing faculties designed to promote good practice in specialised areas of practice. The Neonatal and Paediatric Pharmacists Group is expected to seek the establishment of such a faculty; any standards that subsequently develop from this process would in due course become the standards normally expected in this area of practice. Conversely, any such standards might take many years to become a practice norm and in any event, a 'generalist' on-call pharmacist could not be expected to have specialist expertise in every field where a query may arise.

What guidance does the Code of Ethics give here?

Your key responsibility is to use your knowledge for the wellbeing and safety of patients. You must also ensure that your knowledge is up to date and relevant to your field of practice. Part 2, on the personal responsibilities you carry when offering a service, anticipates the development of specialised areas of practice by requiring you to comply with any accepted codes of practice applicable to your sphere of practice. The Code does not give any specific additional guidance on prescribing for neonates, although in standard 4 there are references to the use of licensed medicines wherever they are available and we have already referred to the specific standards for Patient Group Directions in standard 23. More significantly, in the general introduction to the service specifications, attention is drawn to the need for risk management and assessment procedures to be in place and followed and that adequate records are maintained to enable your service to be monitored. This is a re-statement of the principles of clinical governance which require you to be able to 'know and to show' that your standards of patient care are high. Once again, these requirements mean that before starting work in this job, you should expect an induction process to make sure you are familiar with policies, procedures and documentation relating to the kind of on-call queries you may receive.

What professional knowledge do I have which applies here?

To respond properly to this request, you will need to draw on your existing knowledge of the management of neonates (which may be very limited) and supplement it by reference to the recognised paediatric and neonatal formularies[2] and to *Martindale: The complete drug reference*. As we said in Problem 6, you may want to contact the original prescriber or the neonatal nurse to discuss the reasons for this request and whether there are any alternatives. In the hospital setting, you may have access to the medical notes about the patient and this could inform your understanding of whether or not the supply of an unlicensed drug is the best course for the patient.

Where can I look or who can I ask for advice?

A key factor will be determining how urgent is the need for this medicine. If it is immediate then you have limited options. Is there another pharmacist or consultant who can be contacted for urgent advice at any time?[3] Is there an on-line source of medicines information that might be accessible? If the need is less urgent, or temporary measures can be taken, could you contact your pharmacist or medical colleagues in the morning?

Stage 2: prioritise and ascribe values

Patient, parents, carers

Crucial to your considerations of the interests of the neonate patient will be the consequences of making the supply of an unlicensed medicine or not making such a supply. In either case, you may subsequently be called upon to defend your decision to parents, the hospital and even the wider world. You should at least consider what involvement the parents have had in this prescribing request, if any, and whether they are party to any decisions that may literally be matters of life or death for the neonate. Whilst it may be somewhat remote to your considerations just now, you should be aware of how the hospital operates its consent arrangements in this controversial area of care. Are the parents aware of the consequences of the use of unlicensed medicines and are they comfortable with the measures that may be being proposed?

Other healthcare professionals, your profession

As in Problem 6, this could be a tricky area to address. However, if something went wrong you would be held liable for your part in overseeing the clinical appropriateness of this supply, just as the neonatal nurse and the consultant in charge of the case. Before challenging any request, you will want to marshal all your facts and be ready to substantiate your queries with evidence and to be prepared to suggest alternatives if necessary.

Your employer

We have briefly mentioned vicarious liability in Problem 4 and there is no question that if the worst should happen, your hospital will have in place arrangements to meet any claim for compensation from the patient's parents or other representatives. However, that does not mean you, or indeed your colleagues, would automatically avoid any sanctions in this event. Part of the relationship between employer and employee requires that the employee follows any reasonable policies and procedures put in place by the employer. There may still be a large element of professional discretion, but there is an increasing expectation that the NHS will operate within stated standards, clearly expressed, and monitored and audited accordingly. Of course, the employer must make sure that employees are aware of these policies, etc. and in this case, your line manager should have anticipated such a situation and provided you with a second line contact to a more senior or experienced pharmacist to contact if in difficulty. This process is part of the risk management approach: to anticipate where risks may arise, what could go wrong and develop strategies to respond to them.

Yourself

As in Problem 6, you have a duty to maintain confidence in your profession, and yourself as a member of it, and confidence in other healthcare professionals. However, you must also ensure that no patient is put at risk by the use of unlicensed medicines. Your skill as a competent pharmacist is to carry out this task without alarming the patient's parents or guardians and without antagonising the neonatal nurse or prescriber.

Stage 3: generate options

What *could* you do?

1   Do nothing.
2   Supply without obtaining any further information or advice.

We think you will have little difficulty in recognising that neither of these options is acceptable. They represent the ends of the spectrum of choices and this problem would hardly be a dilemma at all if you could easily choose either option. So what else could you do?

3   Find out sufficient information to satisfy yourself of the clinical appropriateness and then supply.

This may, on the face of it, seem a reasonable option. Certainly, if you were very experienced in neonatal care and were familiar with the drug and neonatal pathophysiology, this may well be a defensible choice. If, however, there were adverse consequences, then your accountability for them might be high.

It is worth adding that if, on the basis of evidence collated, you come to the conclusion that the treatment was inappropriate, then you may exercise professional judgement and refuse to supply. You should be prepared to defend yourself against the consequences of not supplying as well as supplying.

4   Find out sufficient information as in 3, confirm your position with a senior colleague, and then supply.

We did say at the beginning that you should imagine you were a recently qualified and recently appointed pharmacist to this on-call position. As the law expects every practitioner to be competent at whatever professional activity they are performing (or, more correctly, not to undertake activities in which they are not competent), this may be a slightly safer option than 3, if you can secure the necessary confirmation.

Stage 4: choose an option

What *should* you do?

We think you should probably choose option 4; do you agree? Obviously you will want to record what action you took before reaching this decision. Perhaps you could make a note of what references or medical records you checked, what facts you took into account and what colleagues you consulted before reaching your decision. Would you wish or be able to make a note in the patient's medical notes? Is there an agreed policy in the hospital on where such records should be made and in what form and detail? One consequence of working through this problem will be that you are now alerted to the need for risk assessment and working out what you would do on a general basis before the actual problems arise.

Discussion

This problem links an established problem area, the use of unlicensed medicines, with the development of specialised practice. What other areas of specialised practice can you identify, both within hospital and out in the community?

We list a few below and invite you to think how you would prepare to deal with 'unorthodox' or unusual requests in these areas.

- Patients in the intensive care unit.
- Patients receiving palliative care.
- Patients receiving treatment for HIV infection.
- Oncology patients.
- Patients being treated for drug or substance abuse.
- Customers of a private travel health clinic employing pharmacists.

References

1 Patient Group Directions for neonatal use are rare and a pharmacist contemplating supply should contact a senior colleague first. In any event, the pharmacist should expect a copy of the Patient Group Directions to be held in the pharmacy, to be able to consult it personally and possibly consult with the pharmacist who authorised it.
2 For example: Policy Statement from the Royal College of Paediatric Child Health on the use of unlicensed medicines; Royal College of Paediatric Health *Medicines for Children* 1999; Northern Neonatal Network (eds) *Neonatal Formulary*, 3rd edn, 2000; websites www.neonatalformulary.com or www.dial.org.uk.
3 A pharmacist contemplating an on-call position should expect to receive induction training, to have the opportunity to become familiar with the hospital's activities and operations before moving to 'on-call' and to have an 'on-call pharmacist's pack' listing sources of support, with names and contact numbers.

PROBLEM EIGHT

The NHS contract; responsibilities of the superintendent

Try this problem.

The blizzard in the Yorkshire Dales

You are the superintendent pharmacist responsible for a company that owns three pharmacies, all in the Yorkshire Dales. It is February and a blizzard has trapped you in your home when you are supposed to be in charge of one of the pharmacies. Your senior counter assistant, Jean, has arrived, unlocked the pharmacy, and telephones you to ask if she should stay, go or carry on without you. What are you going to do?

What issues should I consider?

- ownership of pharmacies;
- meaning of personal control;
- legal definition of supervision;
- duties of a superintendent;
- NHS Terms of Service, especially 'reasonable promptness' and hours of service;
- key responsibilities of a pharmacist in the Code of Ethics;
- what local knowledge you might have in this situation;

- what knowledge you might have of local healthcare professionals;
- needs of specific patients and the public at large.

Where should I look in Pharmacy Law & Ethics?

- ownership of pharmacies (Chapter 4);
- meaning of personal control (Chapters 4, 21 and 26);
- definition of supervision (Chapters 5 and 21);
- duties of a superintendent (Chapters 4 and 21);
- NHS Terms of Service (Chapter 23);
- key responsibilities of a pharmacist in the Code of Ethics (Chapter 20).

Stage 1: gather relevant facts

What criminal law applies here?

The Medicines Act specifies two conditions in relation to pharmacists and pharmacies. First, a pharmacist must supervise the supply of pharmacy and prescription medicines (Chapter 5) and, secondly, the pharmacy must be under the personal control of a pharmacist. Failure to conduct a pharmacy properly in these two areas is a criminal offence and you as superintendent pharmacist would be personally liable to prosecution as well as the company concerned.

There have been many convictions of pharmacists for failing to supervise adequately, and cases relating to this and failure to exercise personal control have figured quite regularly in the work of the Statutory Committee. You might like to look now at Chapter 21 for examples.

What NHS law applies here?

We said in the introduction to this section that NHS law is administrative law that applies to pharmacy practice; breach attracts financial and administrative sanctions, but not prosecution. Your pharmacies will each have an NHS contract with the local health body which requires them to be open for specified minimum hours or otherwise as agreed with the authority (Chapter 23). Failure to be open for these hours, or indeed failure to supply medicines with 'reasonable promptness', would be a breach of your NHS Terms of Service.

What civil law applies here?

This is difficult to define as only when someone seeks goods or services from your pharmacy could a genuine duty of care be said to exist. Nevertheless, you certainly have a duty to care what happens in your absence and to ensure, as far as is reasonable, that potential patients and customers who would use your pharmacy are not put at risk. Your duties as a manager towards your staff mean that you should take reasonable steps to look after their interests as well.

What guidance does the Code of Ethics give here?

Your key responsibility as a pharmacist is to use your knowledge for the wellbeing of and safety of patients and public. Part 2 of the Code then sets out standards of professional performance. Initially, these standards pick up the need to address the risk management aspects of clinical governance for all services. It is reasonable to expect that you, as superintendent, should anticipate that a pharmacist may be unable to attend at any of your pharmacies and to have some contingency procedures and guidance on what to do in this event. Further standards address your position as the pharmacist intending actually to provide professional services. If you were an employee, for example, you would have a duty to inform the pharmacy owner or some other responsible person as soon as you knew you were unable to honour a commitment to be in charge of a pharmacy.

What professional knowledge do I have which applies here?
Where do I look or who can I ask for help?

We will take these together as it is a little difficult to separate what is technical knowledge from local knowledge. Here you would need to identify what alternative sources of pharmaceutical services were available near your pharmacy. Is your pharmacy the only one in that locality? If so, are there any other pharmacists whom you can call on to replace you, always assuming that they can reach your pharmacy in a reasonable amount of time? Can you move your pharmacists at the other two branches around if your replacement would find it easier to reach one of those rather than your pharmacy?

If there are other pharmacies reasonably close to the one where you were planning to be in charge, are they open and functioning with a pharmacist? Your key responsibilities as a pharmacist in the Code of Ethics require you to work in partnership with other healthcare professionals for the benefit of the public, but we are sure you would anyway.

Can you conduct a pharmacy as a 'drug store' when the pharmacist is not there? No. There are plenty of cases that make this clear (Chapter 21), but someone ought to be at the premises to explain to those customers who do manage to call what alternative arrangements are in place.

What about the doctors in the area? They should be informed of your difficulty and emergency arrangements discussed. Medical practitioners can supply medicines to their own patients in most circumstances, and this may suffice for patients who need medicines for acute conditions (Chapter 8). Do not forget the police or the local hospital – they may be able to deal with urgent cases if necessary.

Finally, you need to assess how long these difficulties may last, both at your home and at the pharmacy. Will facilities be needed to help the staff get home, or stay overnight or share transport? These will be questions for you to handle in your capacity as manager as well as pharmacist.

Stage 2: prioritise and ascribe values

Patient, general public

It is important to ensure that patients and customers know what is going on. However, it is reasonable to assume that they, too, will have difficulty in getting about in the snow and the incidence of truly urgent need for medicines in the community is likely to be quite low, at least for one day's absence. The importance of these concerns will depend on how long it will be before you can resume a full service.

Other healthcare professionals, your profession

We have already covered most of the ground here when you were gathering relevant facts; your fellow professionals will all be expected to work together to sort out some solutions. Are there any contacts in your local RPSGB branch or Pharmaceutical Committee who can help? Is there a local 'cascade' system for circulating information to local pharmacies so that they know of your difficulties? The local radio stations can be very helpful in publicising arrangements for the public in these situations.

Your employer, your staff, yourself

Although members of the public have a right to expect you to rate their interests highly, the safety and comfort of your staff, and indeed yourself, are also important. There is no point in any of them becoming a casualty themselves in an effort to help others.

Stage 3: generate options

What *could* you do?

1   Advise Jean to keep the shop open, but not to sell pharmacy medicines or dispense prescriptions.

2   Advise Jean to close the shop.
3   Advise Jean to keep the shop open, but not to sell any medicines or dispense prescriptions.
4   As 3 but only until a relief pharmacist arrives.
5   Delay and seek further advice.

As always, we should consider risks and probability of the consequences of each action. You might have thought that option 1 was sensible, but it is not lawful (lack of personal control) and puts the staff who are left in the pharmacy in an unenviable position. Option 2 is quite 'safe' from a criminal and civil law perspective, but may create risks for some patients unless you have made alternative arrangements for an alternative source of pharmaceutical services that is easily accessible.

Option 3 is nearly as bad as 1 and might be worse for staff who have to explain why a pharmacy which appears to the public to be 'normal' cannot provide a service. The Medicines Act is somewhat perverse in allowing GSL medicines to be sold from a greengrocer (provided they are in the manufacturer's original container: see Chapter 6) without any control over their sale, while stipulating that the same GSL medicines can only be sold in a pharmacy when there is a pharmacist in personal control. Option 5 is a circular choice that will buy you time before choosing one of the others, but you will not have very long to decide. Option 4 would be acceptable if you could be confident that the staff would obey your instructions and that a pharmacist would be there within, say, an hour or two.

Note that all five options would be a breach of your Terms of Service, although we are unaware of any case being brought in such circumstances. In any event, you should also, as soon as practicable, advise your local health body of your position.

Stage 4: choose an option

What *should* you do?

We think you should choose option 2 if there is a pharmacy nearby and option 4 if you are confident of having a pharmacist there within a couple of hours – provided that the pharmacist is not placed at undue risk and the staff are reasonably comfortable (i.e. warm and dry) in the process. Do you agree?

Discussion

Such situations might arise in a variety of ways, but the questions raised will be similar. You will be balancing the general risk to potential patients and customers against that run by yourself and your staff in struggling to maintain a service. The risk management aspects of clinical governance also mean that you should anticipate the non-availability of pharmacists and other key staff and have contingency plans as to what you would do.

Consider these situations, what you would do and why.

- It is Saturday afternoon and drunken revellers from the local city carnival are invading your pharmacy. Should you close the pharmacy?

- Your pharmacy is a small unit within a large supermarket. Very few of the supermarket staff have made it to work although you have enough staff to cope. The supermarket manager wants to close the premises – what would you do?

- You have managed to open your pharmacy and your staff have struggled through severe rain and gales to be there. Then the power supply fails, which disables your tills, fire and security alarms and your labelling and patient medication record system – what would you do?

- You are about to leave home for your pharmacy when you hear on the news that a bomb has exploded in the town-centre shopping complex that includes your pharmacy. Your dispenser then phones you at home saying she is at the centre and the police will not let anyone near it. She asks you what she should do about the prescriptions, particularly for the three addicts who normally collect their daily instalments at 9.00 a.m. What will you say?

Duty to protect the public, even from pharmacists

Sometimes your duties as a pharmacist can put you in an almost impossible position. Try this problem.

The locum and the bottle of whisky

Your cash supervisor, Anne, tells you that she saw your regular locum pharmacist, Mr W., who covers for your day off, sitting in his car at lunch time, drinking from a whisky bottle. She adds that, the same afternoon, the dispenser told her that Mr W. had made a number of obvious errors when dispensing prescriptions for the nearby mental health day centre. Mr W. is a friend of yours and is not associated with a locum agency. What are you going to do?

What issues should I consider?	■ nature and quality of the medicines supplied; ■ NHS Terms of Service – 'as so ordered'; ■ principles of negligence; ■ key responsibilities of a pharmacist in the Code of Ethics; ■ good practice – management of alcohol abuse; ■ use of outside resources, for example, your professional organisation.
Where should I look in Pharmacy Law & Ethics?	■ nature and quality of medicines (s.64 of the Medicines Act; Chapter 13); ■ NHS Terms of Service (Chapter 23);

- principles of negligence (Chapter 20);
- Code of Ethics (Chapter 20).

First a cautionary note here. Some of the information you have been given is 'hearsay' – Anne is telling you what someone else has said to her. It would be unwise to take any action until you have some first-hand evidence yourself that there is a problem. You should certainly go back to the dispenser to hear her direct account and then see for yourself – perhaps you could drop in unexpectedly after lunch when Mr W. is in charge.

Let us suppose that you are satisfied that there are grounds for concern.

Stage 1: gather relevant facts

What criminal law applies here?

It is not against the law to be 'drunk in charge of a pharmacy'. Nor does Mr W. cease to be a pharmacist in the eyes of the law just because he is drunk or, at least, has been seen to have been drinking. Mr W. can still satisfy the legal requirements to supervise supplies of medicines and be in personal control of the pharmacy. You know, however, that Mr W. drives a car, indeed was seen drinking while sitting in his car, so there would be concerns about his fitness to drive.

Mr W. may, however, fail to prevent errors being made in dispensing. Supplying the wrong medicine is a breach of the Medicines Act legislation (Chapter 13), and a criminal offence, although prosecutions are rarely brought by the RPSGB. If such errors were the result of reckless or irresponsible behaviour (as in this case) rather than human error, then a prosecution might be somewhat more likely and if an error resulted in death, the pharmacist could be charged with manslaughter.

It is worth knowing that convictions of pharmacists are usually notified by the courts to the RPSGB, regardless of whether they occur in a pharmacy context or not (Chapter 21). Thus, a conviction for drink-driving could result in a reference to the Statutory Committee; such matters are for the discretion of the Committee chairman.

What NHS law applies here?

In the same way, the NHS Terms of Service do not include specific conditions about remaining sober, but dispensing a medicine that is not 'as so ordered' by the doctor is a breach (Chapter 23) and could lead to financial and administrative sanctions. The general requirements of employment law are another form of administrative law where power to enforce the provisions rests with employment tribunals.

What civil law applies here?

There are serious civil liabilities incurred by you and Mr W. in this situation. You and he have a duty of care towards the patients and customers who use your pharmacy. Any dereliction of that duty which causes injury or harm will render you both liable for compensation (damages) that reflects the extent of that harm. This may or may not be a higher risk for certain patients (say those with mental health problems) than others.

Set against this is the rather remoter possibility of defamation if you broadcast your suspicions about Mr W. widely and they turn out to be without foundation.

What guidance does the Code of Ethics give here?

The Code of Ethics does not directly prohibit drunkenness or require pharmacists to exhibit sobriety, but the issue is implicit in your key responsibilities as a pharmacist; your duty is to act in the interests of patients and the public. Many cases that have come before the Statutory Committee justify this inference – you might like to look at these now.

Less compelling, but still important, are your key responsibilities to avoid any activity that would impair confidence in the profession or bring it into disrepute. You would also have obligations to help a fellow professional to cope with an apparently serious problem.

What professional knowledge do I have which applies here?

All of your training and experience will tell you that this is an unsafe situation that cannot be ignored. You should check back on the prescriptions that Mr W. has dispensed and take reasonable steps to follow up those that have already been supplied to patients.

Where can I look or who can I ask for help?

The RPSGB has set up two helplines for pharmacists who have problems with drugs, alcohol or stress and for others who wish to get help for those with these problems (Chapter 19). The RPSGB also has its local inspectors, who will probably have experience of this kind of situation and can give you some practical advice. Your employer or the NPA may be able to make some helpful suggestions. In any event, you will want to record your findings in an objective way so that you can justify whatever action you do decide to take. You may also want to take advice on the employment law implications of any action you take, particularly as Mr W. is a regular locum who has not been provided by an agency.

Stage 2: prioritise and ascribe values

Patients, general public

Your first concern must always be protection of the public, if necessary from the actions of a drunken pharmacist. This is a serious but not necessarily urgent matter as you could simply not use Mr W. for a while until you have decided what to do. But then you must consider the consequences of his working in other pharmacies in the same compromised condition and, further, the consequences for Mr W. himself.

Other healthcare professionals, pharmacist colleagues

Whatever your sympathies and sensitivities in a case like this, you cannot allow them to overrule your duty of care to your patients. Nevertheless, this does not mean that you can declare to your professional colleagues that Mr W. is a drunkard. Such an accusation would be unhelpful to him and dangerous to yourself. You would be wise to say nothing specific, but to confine yourself to voicing discreet 'concern' while establishing the extent of the risk that is being created.

Your staff, your employer

Similar considerations will mean that you must be discreet in your observations to staff. You may need to take Anne and your dispenser into your confidence at least and ask them to make notes in writing of their knowledge of Mr W.'s behaviour and performance. If you are an employee, you will have to do the same thing for the benefit of your employer and, as we shall see, for your own protection should the position deteriorate. At the same time, you may want to remind them of their duty not to 'gossip' about this matter, particularly outside work.

Yourself

You may find that your loyalties are split if Mr W. is well known to you or has been a friend to you in the past. Such considerations must not be allowed to obscure your first duty to prevent harm to patients, but must be balanced against your duty to help Mr W. deal with his problems. This is why you must be objective about his condition and make careful observation before jumping to any conclusions.

Stage 3: generate options

What *could* you do?

1   Do not use the services of Mr W. again.
2   As option 1 but tell the RPSGB's inspector about your suspicions.

Option 1 is clearly not a good one because Mr W. may simply go and cause similar problems in another pharmacy. Option 2 is only slightly better, unless you know precisely where Mr W. is going to be working, but is better than nothing. We could add a third option.

3   Keep observing Mr W. and tell the RPSGB's inspector and helpline about Mr W.

This option has merit in that it allows the whereabouts of Mr W. to be known and it anticipates both outcomes of this unfortunate case: either Mr W. will continue to be compromised by his drinking and the RPSGB's inspectors will have to take action to protect the public or he will accept help, in which case you have alerted the people who can provide it. The inspectors may themselves pass information to the helplines, but details are never passed in the other direction.
    There are other options that are worth exploring:

4   Confront Mr W. with your suspicions.

We do not recommend this option unless you are very sure of your facts and have information that will support your accusations. It is a feature of alcohol abuse that sufferers often will not recognise that they have a problem, and if the response is a flat denial you have little room left for manoeuvre. Such a choice might just lead to a change in behaviour in Mr W., but it is more likely to become more covert and lead to Mr W. simply ceasing to do your locums, which leaves you in the position envisaged in option 1.

Stage 4: choose an option

What *should* you do?

Are you expecting us to give you an answer? Such situations are very difficult to deal with. Provided you do not unearth serious and frequent errors because of Mr W.'s condition, we think option 3 would be the best for all concerned – do you agree? If you do uncover serious problems, you may have to take option 2 – dismiss Mr W. but alert the RPSGB's inspector and perhaps the locum agency and local pharmacies as soon as you can.

Discussion

There are many variations on this scenario that you could consider. Here are a few:

- The report you have indicates that Mr W. is abusing controlled drugs rather than alcohol.
- You return to the pharmacy and find that Mr W. is actually incapable and lying on the dispensary floor.
- The report you have talks of Mr W. staggering slightly and having slurred speech but there is no suggestion of alcohol or drug abuse.

Duty to protect the public,

even from pharmacists (2)

In Problem 8, we looked at the consequences of not having available a pharmacist at all to supervise the activities of a community pharmacy. The same issues of public and patient safety would arise in hospital practice if no pharmacist were present, although the law is slightly different. Similar considerations to those in Problem 9 would arise if a pharmacist were available but there were doubts about his or her competence. Try this problem.

The European locum and the hospital staff

You are the pharmacist managing the pharmacy department in a small general hospital. Because of a national shortage of pharmacists, you have had to engage on a one-month trial period, a locum pharmacist, Mr V., to be the sole pharmacist in charge of the dispensary. Your Human Resources department says that occupational health have cleared him for employment and the locum agency has provided evidence that he is registered in Great Britain under reciprocal arrangements within the EU. Two weeks after he starts, your senior pharmacy technician, Sheila, asks to see you. She says that she and other technicians have concerns about Mr V.'s ability to dispense accurately and to carry out proper clinical checks on prescriptions. Moreover, she says she now has a complaint from one of the medical staff and from several patients who say Mr V. cannot converse adequately in English. What action are you going to take?

What issues should I consider?

- offences under the Medicines Act;
- application of Medicines Act to hospital premises;
- registration of pharmacists and relevant bye-laws;
- duty of quality (clinical governance) in hospitals;
- employment law;
- principles of negligence;
- key responsibilities of a pharmacist in the Code of Ethics;
- professional knowledge about the medicines supplied.

Where should I look in Pharmacy Law & Ethics?

- offences under the Medicines Act (Chapter 1);
- application of the Medicines Act to hospital premises (Chapters 2, 8 and 27);
- registration of pharmacists and relevant bye-laws (Chapter 19 and relevant Appendix);
- duty of quality (clinical governance) in hospitals (Chapter 23);
- employment law (Chapter 25);
- principles of negligence (Chapter 20);
- key responsibilities of a pharmacist in the Code of Ethics (Chapter 20).

First a cautionary note as in Problem 9. Some of the information you have been given is 'hearsay'. As well as voicing her own opinions, Sheila appears to be telling you what someone else has told her. It would be unwise to take any action until you have first-hand evidence yourself that there is a problem. Check whether Sheila has some evidence and examples of Mr V.'s alleged incompetence, or whether she has completed any of the hospital's internal 'error or incident' report forms. See if the member of staff or the patients have made written complaints with specific details of when and what exactly is being complained about. Find out whether Mr V. has already been made aware of these complaints and whether any explanations have already been offered. Finally, consider whether the complaints may be biased by a personality clash or cultural prejudices.

Let us suppose you are satisfied that there are grounds for concern.

Stage 1: gather relevant facts

What criminal law applies?

Your priority is firstly to establish the nature and seriousness of any alleged errors made by Mr V. Supplying an incorrectly dispensed medicine is a breach of the Medicines Act (s.64), but more immediately you will want to make sure there is no risk to any patient.

In contrast to the situation in community pharmacy, there is no requirement in criminal law for a pharmacist to supervise the supply of medicines from a hospital pharmacy. However, any such transactions must be part of the business of the hospital and must be carried out in accordance with the directions of a doctor or dentist. For supplies of POMs, these directions must be in writing. So, at least in terms of criminal sanctions, a hospital pharmacy can technically operate without a pharmacist. However, the preparation and assembly of medicines must be carried out under the supervision of a pharmacist to avoid the need for a marketing authorisation or manufacturer's licence. So in practice a hospital pharmacy cannot operate without a pharmacist.

The Pharmacy Act 1954 covers the registration of pharmacists in Great Britain and you may like to look now at the relevant chapter (19) and bye-laws which govern the eligibility to practise in Great Britain of Mr V. and of pharmacists from elsewhere in the world. The reciprocal arrangements with the EU do not allow the Society to test for competence in the English language.

There is another statute which has some relevance to this case: the Public Interest Disclosure Act 1998. This Act aims to protect the right, and indeed duty, of public body employees to raise issues concerning patient or client care, sometimes called 'whistleblowing'. In the past, some individuals have suffered considerable criticism or even abuse for doing just that; in some instances they have found their job prospects halted or have even lost their jobs. Whilst the proper place to raise concerns in the first instance will always be internally, every member of staff in a hospital has a duty to care for the interests of patients.

What NHS law, including hospital service directions, applies here?

The statutory duty of quality placed on trusts by the Health Act 1999 (Chapter 23) requires the trust to implement 'controls assurance' across a wide range of risk areas. The quality of staff will be a possible risk area and your human resources (personnel) department should have operational procedures to manage that risk. In this case, the checks they have carried out on health and registration appear to be part of those procedures, as should be a period of induction training to cope with possibly unfamiliar surroundings. Whilst any sanctions for failing to have adequate risk management controls within the trust may fall on the Chief Executive or other board-level directors, you, as a senior managerial pharmacist, might also be considered accountable for any other measures which you might reasonably be expected to have put in place.

A second area of controls assurance is medicines management. A series of criteria to be monitored have been specified to demonstrate the safe and secure handling of medicines within a hospital. One of these (criterion 11 out of 18 published on the Internet)[1] requires that a pharmacist supervises pharmaceutical dispensing activities. This effectively mirrors the situation that applies statutorily outside the NHS.

The general requirements of employment law are another form of administrative law where power to enforce provisions rests with employment tribunals, both within and outside the NHS.

What civil law applies here?

You have a duty of care to ensure that patients and other users of your hospital dispensary are not put at risk. This duty of care will be heightened as it becomes the norm for hospital trusts to implement controls assurance processes. You also have a duty of care towards your staff to ensure that they are not required to take on responsibilities to which they have not agreed or for which they are not equipped. This may apply to your dispensing technicians who should not have effectively to 'supervise' a pharmacist.

What guidance does the Code of Ethics give here?

Your key responsibility is to use your knowledge for the wellbeing and safety of patients and public. In Part 2 of the Code, on standards of professional performance, section A.1 places responsibilities on locums to only accept work where they have the relevant skills and fitness for the tasks to be performed. Moreover, they should disclose any factors that may affect their ability to provide services. Although this provision is most commonly invoked in areas of conscience, it is equally valid if Mr V. knew that his English was not adequate to cope with the colloquial English he might expect to encounter when dealing with patients. Furthermore, section A.1 expects that if Mr V., or you in his place, considers that because of any mistakes or misunderstandings a patient may have received substandard care, there is an obligation to inform the patient and try to put things right.

You should also note that in section A.2 you have an obligation as a manager to ensure that pharmacists (and other staff) are sufficiently competent in English and to ensure that the Society is informed of pharmacists whose professional competence or ability to practise may be impaired and put the public at risk.

What professional knowledge do I have which applies here?
Where do I look or who can I ask for help?

First, you will need to consider what medications Mr V. has been supplying and the potential for risks to patients arising from errors. You will want to talk this through with Sheila and any other staff who have been working with Mr V. You may want to take advice from more senior colleagues and any member of the staff in the hospital who is generally accountable for risk management. At some stage you may want to contact the Society or the local inspector for their advice. You may consider it wise to take advice from your personnel department before tackling Mr V. directly, particularly in respect of the conditions under which Mr V. was engaged. We look at this in more detail in stage 2. You might also want to know if the locum agency that provided him is aware of any other problems associated with Mr V. and what is their policy in dealing with such situations? Overarching all these questions will be the current availability of other pharmacists. Can you conceivably find a replacement for Mr V.? Would the dispensary have to close if you could not? What other facilities for carrying out its activities might be available?

Stage 2: prioritise and ascribe values

Patients

Your first concern must always be the protection of patients. Are there likely to be any other errors made by Mr V. which have not been made known to the patient? If you were able to find a replacement quickly for Mr V., what might be the consequences for patients of any other pharmacy setting in which he might work?

Mr V. himself

You should pause just a moment to consider whether any of the allegations, or even evidence, against Mr V. might be unfair or even constitute defamation by libel (written) or slander (verbal). Although there are defences to such actions you might want to establish what opportunity Mr V. was given to raise any concerns he might have had about his competence or command of English? Did he ask for any support in carrying out his duties or did he claim to be fully competent from day one? Were the terms of his one-month trial put in writing to him and under what circumstances was it stated that his employment might be terminated?

Other healthcare professionals

The concerns of other healthcare professionals such as the hospital doctor should be acknowledged, but you should be careful about rushing to confirm such concerns. So far, you have heard one side of the story; there may be a number of mitigating factors or exaggerations which will alter the picture quite radically on investigation.

Your staff, your employer

The same restraint upon jumping to conclusions should be exercised with your staff, although you should always take their concerns seriously. It is important that they feel free to identify problems which may affect the quality of the service being given, provided they are prepared to support criticisms with objective evidence. The hospital authority too, will want to be able to show that concerns are noted and some investigation takes place (see reference to 'whistleblowing' in stage 1).

Yourself

Your first duty is to prevent harm to patients, but this must be balanced against your duty to be fair to Mr V. and to deal objectively with the allegations. Dealing with personnel investigations can be stressful, even distressing, for the investigators; you will want to ensure that you alone do not carry the whole burden particularly when issues of employment law are involved.

Stage 3: generate options

What *could* you do?

1   Terminate the use of Mr V.'s services immediately.

We think that you will readily recognise that this is an unsatisfactory option for at least three reasons. First, it may mean that Mr V. will work elsewhere, cause similar problems and be a risk to patient safety; secondly, this will not help Mr V., who may be unaware of his alleged shortcomings but could improve if they were made known to him. Finally, such precipitate action, unless carefully supported, may render the hospital liable for a breach of Mr V.'s employment rights. You will also almost certainly have to explain to the locum agency why you took this action and this may reopen the whole situation once more.

2   After consultation with the locum agency and the hospital personnel department, terminate Mr V.'s employment.

This is clearly a better option, but the time needed to investigate and consult may not address urgent concerns about patient safety. This option also falls short of your duty to ensure that the Society is informed of pharmacists who may be incompetent to practise. So we could add a variation:

3   As option 2, but consult with the Society as well.

In all three of these options, you are losing any opportunity of retaining Mr V.'s services at all. This may open up the prospect of closing down the dispensing facility altogether if you cannot find a replacement. Given the shortage of pharmacists, the cost of recruitment and induction and the possibility that Mr V. may become competent if given some help, what other options might you have?

4   As option 3, but suspend Mr V.'s employment rather than terminate it.

This option has merit because it will ensure that the whereabouts of Mr V. remain known and it provides an opportunity to set in place measures to rectify Mr V.'s shortcomings and keep the option of reinstating him at some time in the future. Any reinstatement may mean quite a lot of work for your staff and/or the locum agency and this may be a factor that will affect your chosen option. It also means that you will still have to find a replacement for Mr V. or contemplate closure of the dispensary. Finally, don't forget that you will have to renegotiate Mr V.'s one-month trial to reflect the changed circumstances.

5   Talk to Mr V. and get his version of events.

This might seem an obvious first option but we would urge you to be careful. Such a conversation needs to be carried out sensitively, using an exploratory approach with a view to clarification and support. An interview could easily become a confrontation and you might prepare for it to become a disciplinary procedure, in a formal interview setting with at least one other representative from the hospital present and a similar facility being offered to Mr V. Even if taking this option did not lead to difficulties under employment law, it may simply result in Mr V. resigning immediately, which will have all the draw-backs of option 1.

6   Bring in an additional pharmacist to support Mr V.

These might be worthwhile options if the availability of pharmacists permits it and you judge that Mr V.'s failings can be managed with further support. You will have to consider what benchmarks you need to establish that this support is effective and, as in option 4, Mr V.'s employment contract will have to renegotiated. This option might fit well with the next, so that specialist pharmacists could be temporarily assigned to the dispensary whilst Mr V.'s difficulties are tackled.

7   Restrict Mr V.'s activities to those of least risk.

It might be reasonable to require that Mr V. does not undertake out-patient or discharge medications but confines his activities to in-patient services. This should mean it is easier to offer support and intermediate safety checks by other healthcare professionals. Alternatively, prescriptions for out-patients could temporarily be written on FP10(HP) or their equivalent for dispensing by community pharmacies.

Stage 4: choose an option

What *should* you do?

We think the overriding factors are maintaining patient safety despite a shortage of pharmacists. All the options mean that you will have to find a replacement or an additional pharmacist in the short term. Given that, we think option 4, followed by options 5, 6 and 7 if practicable would be best – do you agree?

Discussion

The importance of risk management – that is, the process of anticipating risk and having contingency plans to deal with it – is clearly demonstrated in this problem. Whilst this example relates to a locum pharmacist, any pharmacist or indeed any member of the support staff could develop signs of impaired competence and managers should have procedures to deal with that eventuality. When a shortage of essential personnel, such as pharmacists, is anticipated then decisions on what services are dispensable or could be delivered from elsewhere should be taken before the crisis arises rather than afterwards. This is yet another component of clinical governance. What records could you make of this situation and where would such notes be held? Data protection law allows the subject to have access to most data that is held about them, including some parts of personnel data. Even if personnel records are partially protected, you should ensure that any comments or allegations of impaired competence are supported by objective evidence, just as you did before embarking on dealing with the allegations about Mr V.

Consider how you might assess risk and develop strategies to deal with the possibility of:

- A similar situation arising in your 'pharmacy shop' within the hospital which dispenses outpatients prescriptions and sells a small range of over-the-counter medicines.
- Engaging a locum for ward cover on just one day.
- Coping with long-term sick leave in a regular full-time pharmacist.

Reference

1 Website: tap.ccta.gov.uk/doh/rm5.nsf/AdminDocs/CAStandards?OpenDocument.

Duty to protect the public, even from other healthcare professionals

As pharmacists take a more active part in the healthcare team and develop their own unique contribution to patient care, they may come into conflict with the judgements of other healthcare professionals. The following problem is set in the primary care sector, in a GP surgery, but it could equally arise in hospital or community practice.

The contraindication and the confident practice nurse

You are an experienced community pharmacist who has recently started a clinical diploma. As part of the course-work you need to carry out a medication review for a patient with diabetes. You ask the practice nurse at your local surgery, Liz, to select a patient. She suggests Mrs Cooper, an elderly lady who started on insulin a couple of months ago as her diabetes was not controlled by metformin alone.

Whilst reviewing Mrs Cooper's case history you see her creatinine levels indicate mild renal failure at the start of her treatment and that this has become worse although this is not mentioned in her notes. You give a copy of your case review to Liz, draw her attention to the contra-indication and recommend that Mrs Cooper be managed on insulin alone. Liz responds by saying that Mrs Cooper can't possibly manage without the metformin and gives you a clear impression that your recommendation will not be acted upon. What will you do now?

What issues should I consider?
- principles of negligence;
- clinical governance, statutory duty of quality;
- key responsibilities of a pharmacist under the Code of Ethics;
- professional indemnity insurance;
- vicarious liability;
- Data Protection Act;
- reference sources for clinical advice.

Where should I look in Pharmacy Law & Ethics?
- principles of negligence (Chapter 20)
- key responsibilities of a pharmacist in the Code of Ethics (Chapter 20);
- clinical governance, statutory duty of quality (Chapters 20 and 23);
- professional indemnity insurance (Chapters 20 and 23, and Appendix 18);
- vicarious liability (Chapter 25);
- Data Protection Act (Chapter 25).

Stage 1: gather relevant facts

Before any kind of legal or ethical analysis, you will want to be very sure of your clinical facts. Briefly, the use of metformin combined with insulin can be useful to prevent weight gain in obese patients. However, metformin is contra-indicated in patients with renal failure because it can cause lactic acidosis. This is a rare side-effect but it can be fatal. So your first step may be to assemble references to support this clinical information.

What criminal law applies here?

None of the statutes we have so far looked at are at issue here. We should, however, consider the Data Protection Act, which is also discussed in later problems. There is an exemption in the Act which removes the need for patient consent if the information to be shared is necessary for patient care and is shared between healthcare professionals (and any relevant staff) who 'owe a duty of confidentiality'. Strictly speaking therefore, there is no statutory obligation to consult Mrs Cooper before undertaking the review but it is certainly desirable. This is in keeping with the philosophy of the Act to obtain consent to disclosure wherever possible.

We mentioned manslaughter in Problem 9. Where a patient's death can be attributed in any way to a failure of medical care, there is always the possibility of a police investigation to establish whether there are grounds for a prosecution for manslaughter arising from what is usually termed 'criminal negligence'. Such cases are rare, but in 2000 a pharmacist was initially so charged for her part in a dispensing error associated with a death. In such cases, the police may wish to gather evidence which implicates anyone – preregistration pharmacist, dispenser, sales assistant – who may subsequently be judged to have contributed to the death by culpable negligence.

What NHS law applies here?

The Health Act 1999 (Chapter 23) introduced a statutory duty of continuous quality improvement on NHS bodies and services. This is usually termed *clinical governance* and places accountability for the quality of healthcare that professionals give directly or indirectly to NHS patients. In the primary care sector, the ultimate responsibility will rest with the Primary Care Trust Board in England or the equivalent body elsewhere. The individual healthcare professionals, GPs, nurses or those working in association with them, would also carry their own personal responsibilities and be accountable for their actions.

In addition, the same Act introduced a requirement for family health practitioners to hold approved indemnity cover, although, at the time of writing, this has not been incorporated into the pharmacy contractors' Terms of Service.

What civil law applies here?

This situation has a fairly obvious potential to involve you in a medical negligence action. Mrs Cooper's GP would be regarded under the civil law as having the highest duty of care towards Mrs Cooper herself. However, he or she has delegated certain activities to Liz, the practice nurse. Provided the GP is sure that Liz is competent to carry out those delegated tasks, his or her duty of care may be proportionately diminished, but Liz will then acquire a clear duty of care to Mrs Cooper. Now that you as a pharmacist are involved, you will start to acquire a duty of care to Mrs Cooper too.

In a civil action for negligence it is always arguable who exactly and in what proportion the various respondents may carry liability. When dispensing prescriptions, case law now indicates that pharmacists will be held liable, albeit jointly with prescribers, if they fail to intervene when errors could potentially harm patients. It is very likely that the same liability will arise when pharmacists are providing advice on the use of medicines as well as supplying them.

What guidance does the Code of Ethics give here?

Your key responsibility as a pharmacist is to use your knowledge for the wellbeing and safety of patients. This scenario is a clear example of where you have specialist knowledge which must be employed. The Code also says you must work in partnership with other health professions and respect patient's rights to be involved in decisions made about their care. Moreover, your key responsibilities also include an obligation to be up to date and to base your advice on evidence. In part 2 of the Code on standards of professional performance, matching responsibilities are spelled out for both yourself and for your employer (if you are employed) to ensure that all the activities you undertake are covered by professional indemnity insurance.

Professional indemnity is similar to the 'third party' insurance for car drivers. It covers you for the costs of any damage to other persons arising from your faults. If you are employed, your employer will be vicariously liable for the consequences of your actions in the course of that employment. Your employer will normally carry an indemnity insurance arrangement for this purpose, but you should check. If you are self-employed, then you yourself should ensure you are appropriately insured. In this case, you will need to establish whether you are covered by your employment in community practice for this medication review or whether you are temporarily employed by the GP practice and covered by their insurance arrangements.

The Code of Ethics also has more to say on professional competence and confidentiality. In Part 2, paragraph B, guidance specific to your situation is given. Under Part 2, paragraph C, emphasis is again placed on ensuring patient consent to disclosure or sharing of patient information except in closely defined circumstances as set out in the paragraph.

What professional knowledge do I have which applies here?

This is not a textbook on clinical pharmacy so we will not attempt to give comprehensive advice here. The standard textbooks such as the BNF, *Martindale: The complete drug reference* and the *The Medicines Compendium* will contain ample supporting material for your advice. To this you may add national guidance such as (in England) National Service Frameworks and advice from the National Institute for Clinical Excellence (or their equivalents) and any local formularies agreed at practice level or higher. Finally, there are many specialist textbooks on therapeutics which you can turn to.

Where can I look or who can I ask for help?

You could consult the lecturers on your clinical diploma for help in interpreting the facts and information you have found. We have said above that Mrs Cooper's GP carries the prime responsibility for her care, so you might want to speak to him or her. Clearly, this will be much easier if, at the start of your activities in the surgery, you had made yourself known to all the GPs and relevant staff working there. Ideally, an introduction at a suitable practice meeting would have given you an opportunity to explain your background, what your aims were and how you were going to carry them out.

Stage 2: prioritise and ascribe values

Patient

You should have no difficulty in recognising your first priority is Mrs Cooper. If this potential contraindication is not dealt with she could die.

Mrs Cooper's relatives or carers

You may have limited information about Mrs Cooper's personal circumstances, but it is likely that she may have children or other relatives who will be anxious for her welfare. If her condition deteriorates because of a failure to institute avoiding action, then they may hold you accountable along with other healthcare professionals involved in her care.

Other healthcare professionals, your profession

As we suggested in Problem 6 (unlicensed use of Phenergan Elixir) you should prepare carefully before speaking either to Liz or Mrs Cooper's GP. Do you have any alternatives to offer other than simply taking Mrs Cooper off metformin? Be prepared to recognise that they may know more about Mrs Cooper than you and there may be some reasons which are not yet known to you as to why such a change is unwelcome. Be circumspect but firm, bearing in mind your expertise and responsibility as an independent professional.

Employer

We have already said that you should check your position on professional indemnity insurance *before* commencing medication review or similar activities outside you normal employment. Your employers may not be willing to extend their accountability to activities which are completely outside their control.

Yourself

We think this is a good example of where you 'owe it to yourself' to intervene. You are acting as the patient's advocate and seeking to ensure that no treatment which could conceivably cause more harm than good to Mrs Cooper remains uninvestigated. You may eventually reconsider your advice, but you must pursue it as a matter of professional conscience.

Stage 3: generate options

What *could* you do?

1   Do nothing.

You might briefly consider this to be an acceptable option. Mrs Cooper seems to have been maintained so far on this treatment without obvious harm and may continue to be so. Any other patient might have been selected for your medication review and Mrs Cooper's position might not have come to light. We think you should reject this option because once you know that there is a problem, you cannot simply pretend you didn't know. How would you feel if Mrs Cooper did become seriously ill or die?

2   Put your advice in writing to Liz, the practice nurse, but do nothing more.

This might seem marginally safer than option 1 in that you have effectively passed the knowledge to Liz. In fact, it is probably a worse option because you could not subsequently deny that you knew there was a problem.

3   Fully document your advice to Liz and send a copy to Mrs Cooper's GP.

Now you are thinking defensively by involving all the partners in Mrs Cooper's care and ensuring that your advice is backed up by evidence.

4   Ask to see Mrs Cooper.

We have added this option because it highlights the need never to overlook the wishes and needs of the patient. We should always be wary of assuming that an 'elderly' person, or anyone else for that matter, is just a passive partner in their medical treatment. Mrs Cooper undoubtedly knows what her diabetes *feels* like better than anyone else. She may know why she 'can't' manage without metformin or be able to shed light on why Liz has formed this opinion.

Stage 4: choose an option

What *should* you do?

We think we would choose option 3; do you agree?

We have chosen option 3 because we think it is defensible to Mrs Cooper, to her relatives and carers and to the courts if necessary. You would probably add that you would be happy to discuss Mrs Cooper's case if needed and soften the challenge by thanking the practice for letting you undertake this review. Patient care is a partnership, and you must do what is reasonable to ensure that your duty of care is properly discharged and that other healthcare professionals have all the information necessary to meet their duties of care.

Discussion

An important aspect of continuing professional development is the value of *reflective practice* as part of the process of auditing your performance. In other words, to look over the events of the day or a longer period, consider what information and experiences were new to you, what you can learn from them and how you might use this new knowledge to inform your future practice. Most clinical diplomas and other postgraduate studies encourage the keeping of a diary or other record which documents this process. In the future this will be part of the evidence pharmacists will need to show that they are undertaking continuing professional development and of demonstrating their commitment to clinical governance.

Accountabilities of an employee; duties of a superintendent

The non-pharmacist manager and the sales of codeine linctus

You are employed as a part-time pharmacist in a local community pharmacy – one of two owned by a limited company. A non-pharmacist director, Mr M., usually works on the medicines counter and in the rest of the shop. You are suspicious that he is selling large quantities of codeine linctus, especially during your lunch break. What can you do?

What issues should I consider?	■ law relating to ownership of pharmacies; ■ liabilities of non-pharmacists; ■ principles of negligence – remoteness of damage; ■ good practice – management of drug abuse; ■ key responsibilities and standards of professional performance in the Code of Ethics; ■ interests of staff, colleagues and general public.
Where should I look in Pharmacy Law & Ethics?	■ ownership of pharmacies (Chapter 4); ■ liability of non-pharmacists (Chapter 21); ■ negligence (Chapter 20); ■ duties of superintendent (Chapters 4 and 21); ■ Code of Ethics (Chapter 20).

As in Problems 9 and 10, you need to gather some objective evidence before you can decide what to do. You might take note of how many bottles of codeine linctus are on the shelf or in the back before and after your lunch. You might ask the staff casually and discreetly about codeine sales and where the stock seems to have gone, although do not be surprised if they are very well aware of the situation! Let us assume that you have firm evidence to believe your suspicions are justified.

Stage 1: gather relevant facts

What criminal law applies here?

The Medicines Act lays down exactly who can own a pharmacy business (Chapter 4). If the owner is a company, then it must appoint a superintendent pharmacist who is accountable for the management of the business in so far as 'it concerns the keeping, preparing, dispensing and supplying of medicinal products'.

Codeine linctus, being a P medicine, should not be sold at all in your absence unless another pharmacist is present to supervise the sale. Such sales without supervision are criminal offences (Chapter 5) and could result in prosecutions for the company, the superintendent, you and Mr M. This is an unusual state of affairs, whereby Mr M. is subject to the law in his capacity as a director and can be prosecuted as though he were a pharmacist (Chapter 21).

What NHS law applies here?

None. The NHS contract refers only to pharmaceutical services, which do not, at present, include over-the-counter (OTC) sales of medicines.

What civil law applies here?

The consequences of such uncontrolled sales causing injury or damage are significant, even though the purchasers are likely to be pre-existing abusers of drugs. Many will be young people, and there is a real possibility that those near to the drug abuser – parents, relatives, friends – will regard such supplies as contributing to the continuing ill-health of the individual concerned or as a factor preventing him or her from overcoming the addiction. It is not unknown for abusers themselves to contact the authorities and complain that a pharmacist is not properly restricting access to abusable drugs.

What guidance does the Code of Ethics give here?

The issue of how far pharmacists should go in helping drug abusers to manage their addiction has featured heavily in Statutory Committee cases over the years (Chapter 21). You might like to look at these now and see how the profession does not generally expect a pharmacist alone to attempt such a task, other than by refusing to make supplies that are not authorised through a recognised drug rehabilitation programme.

This position is recognised in standard 10 on the sales of P medicines, which says that you, as a pharmacist, must be aware of the abuse potential of certain OTC products and should not supply where there are reasonable grounds for suspecting misuse. You should also be aware of Part 3 of the *Medicines, Ethics & Practice* guide which provides practice guidance. There is a section under 'miscellaneous', called substances of misuse, which helps you identify what kind of products can be abused and in what circumstances.

But this case is not about supply by a pharmacist. You have grounds to believe that Mr M. is making the supplies illegally. As the pharmacist in charge at the material time, you are responsible for those sales, even in your temporary absence.

Take a look at Part 2 of the Code, sections A and B, which are concerned with the personal responsibilities of pharmacists and the particular responsibilities of the superintendent pharmacist. Together, you must ensure that persons who are not pharmacists, like Mr M., are not permitted to assume your responsibilities. This could lead to an uncommon but real dilemma where you have to consider whether you continue in this employment at all if it means compromising your professional judgement and accountability.

Finally, this situation should make you question how the superintendent pharmacist and other pharmacists in charge are complying with the requirements in parts A and B to use trained counter assistants and comply with a protocol for selling non-prescription medicine. Has Mr M. completed an approved training course? Does the protocol (if there is one) not make special provisions for sales of medicines liable to abuse? As the pharmacist in charge, you may modify any existing protocol, say, by insisting that, in future, codeine linctus may only be sold personally by you, although this might cause inconvenience for some bona fide purchasers.

What professional knowledge do I have which applies here?

As in Problem 2, you will know something of drug addiction and how it should be managed. You should know which drugs are likely to be used to supplement a habit and, equally important, which ones are 'fashionable' in the area in which you are working. You will know that consumption of codeine linctus in large quantities will have adverse effects on users, and that this might compromise any long-term supplies that he or she may be obtaining from a drug addiction clinic.

Moreover, such supplies may inhibit or avoid the need to attend such a clinic and leave the abusers to fend for themselves on the 'street', where the quality and safety of misused substances leave a lot to be desired.

Where can I look or who can I ask for help?

You could make discreet enquiries of the staff, who should be aware of what happens when you are out. You could ask other pharmacists who work in the pharmacy whether they share your concerns and you should make your worries known to the superintendent pharmacist. If you feel that such action does not go far enough, or you suspect that other pharmacists are failing to take this aspect of their responsibilities seriously, you might seek advice from the NPA, the RPSGB, your defence association or, in other circumstances, your 'head office'.

Stage 2: prioritise and ascribe values

Patients, contacts

Ultimately, you must do whatever is necessary to prevent patients or customers, including those who are misusing drugs, from being exposed to unnecessary harm. The supply of codeine linctus in an uncontrolled way is harmful, and you must do everything you can to remove your complicity in such activity and to persuade others to do the same. If necessary, you may have to write down your concerns and give reasons, so that you have put others on notice that matters cannot continue; this will serve also to show that you did not simply ignore or withdraw from the problem without trying to solve it.

Other healthcare professionals, your profession

Drug abuse is not, of itself, an offence in the UK, and there are teams of healthcare professionals who are well equipped and well able to minimise the harm that individual drug abusers face. Many drug abusers are not listed with family doctors and do not receive much of the general medical care they would otherwise have. When drug abusers attend a clinic, there is at least the opportunity to intervene in healthcare problems and to move abusers from the more harmful routes of abuse to others that cause less harm. Any failure to supervise adequately the sale of abused medicines is not only a breach of the law; it may also bring, as in this case, disrepute upon the profession as a whole.

Your employer, staff and colleagues, yourself

Mr M. is not, strictly speaking, your employer, but both he and your superintendent pharmacist function in a similar way in their dealings with you. If it is your 'employer' who is behaving improperly, then your responsibility towards him or her and your duty to protect his interests diminishes considerably. You will have a duty to do what you can to prevent the pharmacy staff being put in a difficult position and to encourage your pharmacist colleagues to take their own measures to discharge their responsibilities.

Stage 3: generate options

What *could* you do?

1 Do nothing and continue with your part-time work.
2 Do nothing and seek other employment.

Of these, option 1 is not only unacceptable from the patients' point of view, in that it continues to place them at risk, but you are also compromised by going along with a situation that you know to be wrong. Option 2 removes the latter risk but is still inadequate where the patients' interests are concerned.

3 Confront Mr M. and insist that he stops.

This is not a bad idea if you are sure of your facts. It is just possible that he does not know what the law requires – although the superintendent pharmacist should have told him – and quite possible that he does not know what addicts use to supplement their drug habits. But this still means that the superintendent and other pharmacists are either unaware of, or think they do not need to worry about, what has been happening.

4 As option 3, but also write down your position and the reasons for it and raise the matter formally with the superintendent pharmacist.

This is better than option 3 because you are protecting your position as well as trying to do something about the situation. Need you go further? What if others, such as staff or pharmacists elsewhere, have noticed illegal or excessive sales of codeine linctus and tell the RPSGB? This is not uncommon. We think that there is yet more you should do.

5 As option 4, but also contact the RPSGB and tell the RPSGB's inspector or the local drug squad officer what has been happening. You should be able to do this without the source of the information becoming publicly known.

In theory, this might be risky while you were still the pharmacist in charge of the pharmacy, because, if you go back to stage 1, under criminal law, offences that could be the subject of prosecution have been taking place. You must set against this risk your conscience as a pharmacist and the further risk that the offences may continue; you may then be involved at a later stage and asked to justify why you failed to take adequate steps to prevent this.

Stage 4: choose an option

What *should* you do?

Not much difficulty here as we hope we have made the case for option 5 – do you agree?

Discussion

This case illustrates that, although liability to prosecution lies only with the owner of the pharmacy business and directors, professional liability applies to all pharmacists when they are in charge of a pharmacy, even though they might not be physically present during lunch times or tea breaks. Staff working in a pharmacy must understand the limits of what they are permitted to do in law, and that includes non-pharmacist directors. The superintendent pharmacist in particular must repeatedly make this clear to those affected.

There are many other 'irregularities' that you might come across. What might you do in these situations?

- You become aware that a fellow employee pharmacist is helping himself to dispensary stock – you think that it includes diazepam and temazepam.
- You discover a member of staff regularly allowed to 'borrow' against her next prescriptions, which do not seem to arrive.
- You become aware that several members of staff are supplying codeine linctus freely because (a) they are being threatened with violence and feel intimidated or (b) one of them has a boyfriend among the local drug users.

PROBLEM THIRTEEN

A matter of confidentiality

With the almost universal use of computerised patient medication records and closer working relationships with other healthcare professionals, pharmacists are acquiring significant quantities of sensitive data that are related to identifiable individuals. Try this problem.

The suicide and his girlfriend

A young man and his girlfriend, Miss Wright, bought a house together on an endowment mortgage, but three years after moving in the young man committed suicide. Miss Wright notified the insurance company, which demanded further information about the man's medical history before agreeing to pay on the policy. She comes into your pharmacy, tells you all this and asks for a printout of her boyfriend's medicines for the last three years.

What issues should I consider?

- Data Protection Act;
- Access to Health Records Act;
- ownership of NHS records;
- duty of confidentiality;
- principles of defamation;
- key responsibilities of a pharmacist in the Code of Ethics, specific guidance on confidentiality;
- pathology – consequences of disclosure;
- use of outside resources, for example, employer, professional organisation;
- urgency of need.

Where should   ■   data protection issues (Chapter 25);
I look in   ■   confidentiality, defamation (Chapter 20);
Pharmacy
Law & Ethics? ■   Code of Ethics (Chapter 20).

Stage 1: gather relevant facts

What criminal law applies here?

The Data Protection Act 1998 (Chapter 25) covers all information, whether computerised or held on paper, that relates to an identifiable, living human being. It sets out eight principles, which cover the proper management of this 'personal data'; breaches of which are criminal offences. In this instance, you have to be sure of who owns, and therefore controls access to, this data and that you can lawfully disclose the information requested. The Act makes clear the accountability of the person or organisations that processes the data, i.e. the 'data controller'. In community pharmacy, patient medication records are the property of the pharmacist or pharmacy company that holds them. Contrast this with the hospital and GP service, whose medical records (which include medication details) are generally accepted to be the property of the local health body. The Act also defines the accountability of the 'data processor' – which is you.

Records relating to patients kept by pharmacists are additionally 'health records' as defined under the Access to Health Records Act 1990 (Chapter 25). Although this Act is mostly repealed by the Data Protection Act 1998, it retains provisions relating to access to health records after the patient's death. The Data Protection Act no longer applies after the death of the data subject, but other obligations continue when the record is a health record.

What NHS law applies here?

There are no requirements in the Terms of Service to keep patient medication records. However, to qualify for certain payments under the NHS Terms of Service, there are some provisions in the Drug Tariff as to what they should contain.

What civil law applies here?

Disclosure, or failure to disclose, will not result in physical injury or damage to Miss Wright, still less to her boyfriend. But physical injury is not the only kind of damage. You still have a duty to care for the interests of your patient, even after death, which includes an obligation to keep confidential information that you have acquired about him in the course of your practice. The patient's family and close contacts may suffer distress and embarrassment if the records are freely disclosed – this can also be classed as 'damage', for which compensation can be sought. Miss Wright may suggest that she is incurring unnecessary costs for every month that she has to go on meeting the mortgage until the insurance company pays out. These costs may also be classed as 'damage'. Finally, although this is unlikely with pharmacy records, rude or personal comments that may have been kept in medical records for the information of the holder may be considered defamatory if disclosed. This may result in more grounds for claiming compensation.

What guidance does the Code of Ethics give here?

In the standards of professional performance (Part 2), there is a special section spelling out your common law and professional obligations to protect the confidentiality of the records you hold. It goes much further in spelling out circumstances when you might disclose, the most obvious one being where you have the consent of the patient. It also says you can disclose to someone who has a statutory (legal) right to such information.

What professional knowledge do I have which can help here?

You should check the record to see if it discloses evidence of serious conditions, such as HIV infection or cancer, which may cause distress if disclosed. In this case, there might well be evidence of a mental health condition of which Miss Wright may be quite unaware. You should also assess whether there is evidence of prescribing or dispensing errors that, in other circumstances, may be the reason for the request. You should bear in mind the consequences for you and the recipient if this information is disclosed.

Where can I look or who can I ask for help?

If you are an employee, your employer may have a policy and procedures for dealing with requests such as this. Such data may also be commercially sensitive and covered by your general obligation as an employee not to give away your employer's commercial secrets. This is a tricky area and you may want to check with the RPSGB, the NPA or your defence association.

Stage 2: prioritise and ascribe values

Patient

You have a duty to act in the interests of your patient, even when dead. You may have known him well and had an understanding of what he might have wished to happen were he alive. More likely, you will have no insight into this area at all.

Patient's parents, next of kin

You may wish to know whether Miss Wright is the next of kin or whether the deceased's parents are still alive and may have a prior claim to this information. Have the patient's relatives consented to this disclosure? Who has a financial interest here and what would your position be if you contributed to some fraudulent claim under the insurance?

Other healthcare professionals, your profession

We have already hinted that you should be alert to the possibility that the records may be valuable evidence in a medical negligence case. Has the patient's doctor been approached with the same request? As we said in Problem 2, you have a duty not to be gullible and to at least consider the possibility that Miss Wright is not who she says she is or that she is not telling the truth. What evidence does she have of her identity and the truth of her story?

Your employer

In this case, the employer would have vicarious liability for your actions and would probably be considered to be the true owner of the patient medication records. You must therefore consider your employer's interests and involve them in your decision.

Yourself

As well as ensuring that you are not yourself at risk from your actions, you may have your own views on the propriety of this claim. Insurance claims are often invalidated by suicide; should this concern you? Do you think it fair that Miss Wright should collect the money? You might also want to think about the means of suicide. If it had been from an overdose, are there any implications for you as the supplier of the medicines or for the prescriber?

Stage 3: generate options

What *could* you do?

1   Refuse to supply the printout to Miss Wright.
2   Require a court order before you will disclose to Miss Wright.

Both of these options, if unhelpful, may seem 'safe'. In fact, they could be unlawful because Miss Wright may have a legal right to see these records. Have a closer look at the requirements of the Access to Health Records Act and you will see that there is a provision whereby anyone who has a claim arising out of a patient's death can require access to the patient's health records. So we had better not choose options 1 or 2.

3   Require a request in writing from Miss Wright, stating authority for claim and precise details required.

4　　Require a request in writing from the insurance company giving precise details of what is required and why.

5　　Require a request in writing from the parents or next of kin authorising disclosure.

Now you are thinking hard! And you are thinking defensively, which is increasingly appropriate in modern pharmacy practice. But there is another option, which we said was always worth considering:

6　　Delay and pass the query to your employer, head office or defence association, or seek direct legal advice.

Stage 4: choose an option

What *should* you do?

We think you should choose option 6 – do you agree?

There is no great urgency to this request, and you need time to check the veracity of Miss Wright's story. You also need time to check on your knowledge of the Access to Health Records Act – you may exclude disclosure of information that you consider to be irrelevant to the claim for access or which you think could cause serious harm to the physical and mental health of any individual. You do not even have to inform Miss Wright that you have done this although, of course, you could be challenged on your actions at a later stage.

This has some relevance to the form of information you might supply to Miss Wright. She asks for a printout; not every computer system can provide these, or let you make amendments. It would look very unprofessional if certain parts of the record had been manually obliterated because you thought they were unsuitable. It is probably a better idea to create a letter providing the information you have selected together with any clarifications that you feel are necessary. The legislation allows that the provision of information need not be immediate; you would expect to have time to make reasonable enquiries.

Finally, but importantly, options 3, 4 and 5 all suggest written requests for information.

Taking your time, asking plenty of questions and recording everything is the hallmark of the professional who can show that he or she is taking 'all reasonable steps' to discharge their responsibilities conscientiously (see the professional decision-making section).

A matter of
confidentiality (2)

The concept of confidentiality is far wider than the requirements of the Data Protection Act. It a fundamental part of healthcare ethics and is now implicit in the Human Rights Act 1998 provisions which establish a legal right to respect for private and family life. Providers of healthcare have always reasonably argued that patients will withhold sensitive but possibly vital information from their doctors, nurses, etc. if they cannot be confident that such details remain private. Whilst total privacy has to be balanced against certain statutory or public interest arguments for disclosure, the best rule in cases of uncertainty is to secure the patient's consent to disclosure. To be valid, the patient must be capable of understanding the implications of giving consent (known as having 'capacity' to give consent) and be given as much information as is needed to ensure this understanding ('informed consent'). There is no legal obligation to have written records of consent, but in some instances this is a wise precaution.

(It is beyond the scope of this book to give guidance on mental health law which covers the position of patients who lack capacity to give consent. Interested readers may wish to consult the Further Reading suggested at the end.)

The friend in hospital and her anxious mother

You are a clinical pharmacist working in a psychiatric hospital. On a routine ward visit you are surprised to see a longstanding friend, Emma, has been admitted. After chatting briefly you continue the ward round.

As you are leaving about half an hour later Emma's mother whom you also know confronts you outside the ward. Emma's mother is very agitated and demands to know what is wrong with Emma, what is she taking and when will she be well again? What will you do?

What issues should I consider?

- Data Protection Act;
- Health Service Circulars in the NHS;
- principles of negligence; breach of confidentiality;
- key responsibilities of a pharmacist in the Code of Ethics;
- nature of Emma's condition and treatment.

Where should I look in Pharmacy Law & Ethics?

- Data Protection Act (Chapter 25);
- Health Service Circulars in the NHS (Chapter 27);
- principles of negligence; breach of confidentiality (Chapter 20);
- key responsibilities of a pharmacist in the Code of Ethics (Chapter 20).

Stage 1: gather relevant facts

What criminal law applies here?

The Data Protection Act 1998 would apply to all data concerning Emma's condition, so her medical records, treatment details and care plan, for example, are clearly controlled by this Act. The Act also goes on to control consultation and use of such data, so even verbal communications using this information without consent could conceivably be a breach of the Act. The Data Protection Act provides an exemption whereby disclosure of information is permitted if it is necessary for medical purposes and is to a healthcare professional or a member of their staff who is bound by a duty of confidentiality; this exemption would not extend to relatives.

What NHS law, including hospital service directions, applies here?

In 1997, a government report, under the chairmanship of Dame Fiona Caldicott, considered the controls needed over the transmission of patient information within the NHS. Subsequently, an NHS Health Service Circular (HSC 1999/012) required all hospitals to designate a 'Caldicott guardian' whose duties included the institution of processes and controls to ensure that the minimum of information about patients was transferred within the service and that appropriate safeguards were in place to ensure this information only reached its intended recipients. A further Circular (HSC 2000/009) reminded hospitals that they were subject to the provisions of the Data Protection Act. Your interview and particulars of employment should have included agreement to the maintenance of confidentiality. You should be aware of what policies and procedures your hospital has in place over the confidentiality of patient information and what guidance, if any, is given to address this particular situation. This may be a useful source of defence if you decide that you cannot help Emma's mother.

What civil law applies here?

Disclosure of Emma's details to her mother may not result in physical injury to Emma but this is not the only kind of damage, which can attract compensation for a breach of duty of care. Anxiety or distress caused by careless disclosure of patient's details could still be regarded as negligent. Even if disclosure without consent did not lead to an action of this nature, it might conceivably jeopardise Emma's progress or treatment and this could result in measurable injury. Finally don't forget that 'damage' can also include financial loss such as loss of earnings caused by delay in Emma's return to work.

What guidance does the Code of Ethics give here?

Your key responsibilities as a pharmacist explicitly include reference to respect for patients' confidentiality and patients' rights to participate in decisions about their care. In addition, a specific section, Part 2, section C, of the Code gives detailed guidance of just when the law or public interest might be presumed to override the usual absolute need to ensure the consent of the patient to any disclosure of information about them. Interestingly, this section does not include the fairly obvious situation where patient information needs to be shared between healthcare professionals or carers who need this information to provide their contribution to the overall care of the patient. This may be because of the exemption referred to under the criminal law described above.

What professional knowledge do I have which can help here?

In your position as a clinical ward pharmacist you will have knowledge of Emma's condition and treatment. You may also have specialised knowledge of the pharmaceutical care of psychiatric patients, but this would not increase your duty of confidentiality. This would not vary with the amount of information you have, only its nature. Contrast this with the heightened duty of care you would have in the care of neonates mentioned in Problem 7.

Where can I look or who can I ask for help?

We have already mentioned the probability that your hospital has procedures governing the disclosure and sharing of sensitive patient information. You will have colleagues on the medical and nursing teams who may be able to provide background or respond to Emma's mother's demands for information.

You may also have access to Emma's full medical record, although this may depend on the hospital's policy.

Stage 2: prioritise and ascribe values

Patient

Quite clearly, it is Emma whose interests and wishes must prevail in this situation. She has capacity to give consent; you know this because you have talked to her. So there is no reason why she cannot be consulted.

Patient's parents, carers, friends

In some ways your professional knowledge might be a handicap in dealing with her mother's demands since you may be aware that Emma has perhaps a serious condition with a poor prognosis. Your instincts may tell you that her mother should be similarly aware so that she can help and support Emma. However, these sentiments should be resisted since Emma is an adult and competent before the law to manage her own affairs. Nevertheless, you should consider what support you could give her mother short of actually disclosing details about Emma's condition. Perhaps you can offer her a chair and a cup of tea and try to establish what exactly her fears are and how much she knows already.

Other healthcare professionals, your profession

The consultant and other doctors or nurses caring for Emma may already know how much or how little information Emma wants her mother to have. You might expect to discuss Emma's case with your colleagues, but bear in mind that such sharing of information must be within the bounds of the Data Protection Act exemption. It would not be appropriate, for example, to discuss the case at home with your spouse.

Your employer

Your trust hospital would be vicariously liable if your actions led to a civil action. Hospitals and other bodies in the public eye are vulnerable to criticism by the media so you will want to be sure that your actions are defensible to a wider world, as well as within the hospital itself.

Yourself

You may find yourself in a true dilemma because of your wish to do as Emma wishes and to relieve her mother's distress. You now have enough facts and priorities to decide what to do.

Stage 3: generate options

What *could* you do?

1   Tell Emma's mother what you know.

We think we have established why this simply is not a defensible option. It would be a breach of confidentiality, a breach of your professional ethics and the law and could have serious consequences for yourself and the hospital, and possibly for Emma.

2   Tell Emma's mother you cannot discuss the matter at all.

This option is certainly safe but is hardly a proper response for a pharmacist. Emma's mother is distressed and you should try to address that as we suggested in stage 2.

3   Take time to sit with Emma's mother and explain why you can't divulge the information she wants, and then decide what further action to take.

Stage 4: choose an option

What *should* you do?

We think this is a fairly easy choice to select option 3 – do you agree?
    There are various follow-up actions which may result. You might suggest that Emma's mother speaks to the consultant in charge, but this may just shift the dilemma away from yourself. The consultant may not know Emma's wishes and Emma's mother may become even more distressed by a second refusal to respond to her. Emma's mother may also have tried to secure this information from the consultant before.
    You might suggest that Emma's mother should speak to Emma herself about her concerns. Unfortunately, this may cause distress to Emma if she is already struggling with a difficult diagnosis or coming to terms with her condition. Moreover, not all daughters get on with their mothers and vice versa, so you may just be precipitating some conflict that may make matters worse.

You might volunteer to talk to Emma on her mother's behalf.

This is somewhat similar to the 'buy time' option that we suggest you always consider. There is no true urgency to provide this information; it will not change in a matter of hours. The urgency is to deal with the mother's distress. You will also have to prepare Emma's mother for the possibility that Emma will not give consent to reveal any more information.

Discussion

Would you think this incident is worth recording and, if so, where? If you believe an incident may have later repercussions or will be needed by other professionals dealing with Emma's care (and we think both are likely), you should make a signed, dated and timed entry chronologically in Emma's notes. This might be particularly important if you find that although Emma does not want her illness discussed with her mother, she subsequently becomes unable to manage her treatment and suffers adverse events which her mother might have been able to prevent has she been given more information about Emma's condition.

You might like to consider what other options and issues might arise:

- if the patient is under 16;
- if the patient has just been told she has terminal cancer;
- if the patient is incapacitated through mental illness.

Further Reading

Information on the legal ramifications of confidentiality, consent and mental health law may be found in:

Montgomery J. *Health Care Law*. Oxford: Oxford University Press, 1997.
Mason J. K., McCall Smith R. A. *Law and Medical Ethics*, 5th edn. London: Butterworths, 1999.

PROBLEM FIFTEEN

Private beliefs and
patients' needs

Pharmacists in community practice do not often have to grapple with their private beliefs in the course of their everyday practice. As medical practice, and the pharmaceutical practice that complements it, makes progress, issues surrounding the concepts of the beginning and end of life are increasingly likely to be raised and actions called into question. Try this problem.

The adolescent girl and the Levonelle

Your pharmacy is in the heart of a major city and is open for long hours, seven days a week. You do the late shifts and many of your regular customers are 'clubbers' whom you have got to know personally. It is Good Friday, it is 7.00 p.m., and one of your regulars, who calls herself Deedee, comes in to ask if you can supply her with some Levonelle tablets. She has had them before from the sexual health clinic within the local hospital. She tells you she had a wild night with a group of boys last night, had unprotected sex and the clinic does not open until Easter Tuesday. What will you do?

What issues should I consider?

- criteria for making an 'emergency supply';
- use of Patient Group Directions;
- the principles of negligence;
- key responsibilities of a pharmacist in the Code of Ethics;
- personal responsibilities when providing professional services;

- action, uses and conditions of marketing authorisation for Levonelle;
- use of outside resources, for example, reference books, local support services.

*Where should
I look in
Pharmacy
Law & Ethics?*

- 'emergency supply' (Chapter 7);
- Patient Group Directions (Chapters 7 and 8)
- negligence (Chapter 20);
- Code of Ethics (Chapter 20).

Before embarking on this problem, you should ensure you know about Levonelle. At the time of writing, this medicine exists in two forms: Levonelle-2, a POM and Levonelle, a P medicine. Look up their details to see how the conditions of marketing vary. One crucial piece of information will be Deedee's age. She eventually tells you that she is 14.

Stage 1: gather relevant facts

What criminal law applies here?

We have covered the requirements for 'emergency' supply in Problems 1 and 2. Provided that you could establish from your patient medication record or by some other means that Deedee has previously had Levonelle prescribed, and you know the dose, you could decide that the 'emergency' supply provisions apply, but this does not seem likely in this case. Much more likely, however, is that this is not a simple question of whether to make an 'emergency supply' of a POM. Deedee probably received Levonelle-2 without a prescription under the terms of a Patient Group Direction at the hospital.

We have seen in Problems 6 and 7 that if a P medicine is supplied for use in circumstances outside its marketing authorisation, the product will be controlled as a POM. Knowingly to supply Levonelle, which is authorised only for supply to patients of 16 or over, to a young girl who is under 16 could be an offence under the Medicines Act.

What NHS law applies here?

It is also possible that a Patient Group Direction may be in place locally setting out how emergency hormonal contraception might be supplied from certain pharmacies. If this were the case, then any pharmacist who makes such supplies does so within the terms of a contract with the local health body that drew up the Patient Group Direction. This has implications for liability, if the pharmacist goes outside the terms of the Direction but also gives scope to supply Levonelle-2 free of charge within the NHS (where a prescription levy would not apply) and also under the wider marketing authorisation conditions of Levonelle-2.

What civil law applies here?

You have a duty of care towards all your patients, including Deedee, regardless of their lifestyle or how they came to be in need of your help. However, that is some way from saying that if you do not help you could be liable for the consequences. Rather more likely, unfortunately, is that you may be held liable for any adverse effects arising from the use of Levonelle, if you do supply it. One issue to consider is Deedee's age. In Scotland, the law on the age at which minors (young people) can give consent to treatment is taken to be when in the opinion of a qualified medical practitioner the patient is capable of understanding the nature and possible consequences of the procedure or treatment. A similar position was reached in England and Wales in a test case brought by a Mrs Gillick against a health authority; this is now usually referred to as demonstrating 'Gillick competence' or applying the 'Fraser ruling' – Lord Fraser being one of the judges hearing the case.[1,2] This interpretation has come to apply to the judgement of any healthcare professional who is involved in dealing with young people. Do you think that Deedee is likely to continue to have unprotected sex and/or that her health might suffer if she does? Do you think she will understand any advice that you give her? Do you think she can be persuaded to tell her parents of her difficulties? These are some of the questions you should consider when assessing Deedee's competence to make best use of Levonelle.

What guidance does the Code of Ethics give here?

The Code anticipates that some pharmacists may have religious or personal convictions that direct them not to be involved in the supply of products for the control of pregnancy, conception or termination of pregnancy. In Part 2 of the Code, on standards of professional performance, there are matching obligations for individual pharmacists and their managers. You will see that pharmacists are expected to make known to their employer or manager if any such reservations may affect their willingness to undertake certain services and their employer or manager must make arrangements to accommodate those reservations. However, the Code makes it clear that, even if this does apply to you, you must make every effort to help individuals who need such products, including advising them of an alternative source of supply if necessary. Moreover, this must be done in a discreet and non-condemnatory manner that fully protects the patient's right to confidentiality. Remember that Part 2 C of the Code also makes it clear that you should not normally disclose any patient information to others without consent.

Additionally, the Code has a specific standard, number 11, which applies to the supply of emergency hormonal contraception. This makes it clear that you should deal with the request personally and should offer advice on regular methods of contraception, disease prevention and sources of help.

What professional knowledge do I have which applies here? Where can I look or who can I ask for advice?

Levonelle is not a product with serious side effects but it is not intended as a method of regular contraception. Looking at the textbooks – *Martindale: The complete drug reference, The Medicines Compendium,* the BNF and in literature published jointly by the RPSGB and the Family Planning Association – will give you the details. This is a supply over which you must take particular care and, if you do decide to supply, make a record of the care that you took. Because of the sensitive nature of the use of Levonelle, The Centre for Pharmacy Postgraduate Education run courses and produce training booklets on how to deal with difficult requests such as this one. In addition, the *Pharmaceutical Journal* of 20 January 20 2001 included a practice checklist outlining key points to bear in mind before making a supply and summarising what advice to give.

You will want to ask Deedee if she is taking other medication and, if so, assess whether this will compromise the effectiveness of the Levonelle. You will know that Levonelle should be taken as soon as possible after coitus, but will be effective for up to 72 hours afterwards. You may be aware of the availability of doctors over the Easter holiday period who will be better equipped than you to deal with the request if Deedee has some medical contra-indication. If Levonelle is contra-indicated, one option might be the temporary fitting of an intrauterine device. Even if the surgeries are closed, many local family planning clinics offer emergency helplines and emergency clinics, especially in the major conurbations.

Stage 2: prioritise and ascribe values

Patient, dependants

It is probably very important to Deedee that she does not become pregnant, but she must be fully involved in the decision to use Levonelle and encouraged to understand the limitations and precautions involved. You must explain the possible consequences and ensure that they are understood.

Your duty as a pharmacist is to do that which is in the interest of the patient, but to do this properly you will have to spell out the limitations on what you can do and be sure that Deedee understands these and the possible consequences, say, if she is already pregnant or if the Levonelle fails and an ectopic pregnancy results.

Patient contacts

You may think it right to enquire as to what method of protection Deedee uses and explore what risks she and her contacts may incur.

Other healthcare professionals, your profession

Given the special nature of this request, you could suggest to Deedee that she should consider consulting her doctor or a clinic that can provide any supporting supplies or advice. If Deedee does not want anyone else informed, including her parents, you must respect that wish.

Yourself

The guidance from the Society does not require you to keep records of supply of Levonelle as a P medicine, although supplies under a Patient Group Direction may do so. You should consider whether, in this case, you should take steps to protect your own position by writing down what you have done and why and, ideally, getting written confirmation from Deedee that she has understood and accepts the matters you have discussed. If you decide to supply outside the marketing authorisation, you may be liable for the consequences unless you can point to the steps you took to do your best for the patient (see Problems 6 and 7).

We have not yet contemplated the likelihood that you may not think it right to supply Levonelle to individuals such as Deedee, or even to supply it at all. As we said above, such a position would be covered by your personal responsibilities under Part 2 of the Code of Ethics, which says that if you are of this mind you must nevertheless make every effort to ensure that Deedee receives the help she needs.

Stage 3: generate options

What *could* you do?

1   Say that you cannot supply the Levonelle.
2   Delay and seek advice.

At first sight this might seem a little unhelpful, as speed is important if Deedee is to be helped. What we are thinking of is a short delay for you to make arrangements to speak to Deedee quietly and calmly, and that might involve asking her to come back in, say, half an hour when you are less busy and have time to ensure that she fully understands the situation, go through the patient leaflet with her and advise on contraception methods. You yourself may also need this time to find out which local pharmacies, if any, are trained and prepared to supply Levonelle under a Patient Group Direction. But you will still have to decide what to do then. We think that you have two further options left:

3   Do everything you can to arrange for Deedee to be seen by a doctor or at the sexual health clinic.

In the past, when Schering PC4 was the only available form of emergency contraception, this may have been the best option. It still could be if Deedee has some medical contra-indication to using Levonelle. But we think this is rather unlikely and, in any event, would have to be balanced against the importance of using Levonelle within 72 hours of unprotected intercourse to be confident that it will be effective.

4   Supply Levonelle and keep full written records of what you explained and confirmation of Deedee's understanding.

Stage 4: choose an option

What *should* you do?

We think that option 4 may well be the best option for Deedee, but you would have to be prepared to defend your decision – do you agree? You should certainly try option 3 as well and do your best to persuade Deedee to be seen by a doctor or in a clinic; perhaps you might offer to help her make the appointment.

Discussion

There are some thought-provoking variations to this scenario.

- What if you suspect that the person seeking the Levonelle has been coerced into having sex or is showing other signs of sexual abuse?
- What if you have already made similar supplies to Deedee in the recent past?
- What if a young man comes in making a similar request for his girlfriend?
- What if a request is made in anticipation of unprotected sex?
- What if you think that there is a widespread problem in the area with the clubs and the effect they have on young people's behaviour? Should the RPSGB's inspector or the police be informed? Or the local family planning service or sexual health clinic? What about the implications for the spread of sexually transmitted diseases?

References

1 Editorial. *Pharm J* 23 March 1985 p. 354.
2 Editorial. *Pharm J* 11 May 1985 p. 589.